SECURE PARENT, SECURE CHILD

How a parent's adult attachment
shapes the security of the child

MIROLAND IMPRINT 40

Canada Council   **Conseil des Arts**
for the Arts   **du Canada**

ONTARIO ARTS COUNCIL
CONSEIL DES ARTS DE L'ONTARIO
an Ontario government agency
un organisme du gouvernement de l'Ontario

Canadä

Guernica Editions Inc. acknowledges the support of the Canada Council
for the Arts and the Ontario Arts Council. The Ontario Arts Council
is an agency of the Government of Ontario.

We acknowledge the financial support of the Government of Canada.

SECURE PARENT, SECURE CHILD

How a parent's adult attachment shapes the security of the child

Annette Kussin
M.S.W., R.S.W., Psychotherapist

MIROLAND (GUERNICA)
TORONTO • CHICAGO • BUFFALO • LANCASTER (U.K.)
2023

Guernica Founder: Antonio D'Alfonso

Connie McParland, Michael Mirolla, series editors
Michael Mirolla, editor
Cover design and typsetting: Rafael Chimicatti
Interior design: David Moratto
Guernica Editions Inc.
287 Templemead Drive, Hamilton, ON L8W 2W4
2250 Military Road, Tonawanda, N.Y. 14150-6000 U.S.A.
www.guernicaeditions.com

Distributors:
Independent Publishers Group (IPG)
600 North Pulaski Road, Chicago IL 60624
University of Toronto Press Distribution (UTP)
5201 Dufferin Street, Toronto (ON), Canada M3H 5T8
Gazelle Book Services
White Cross Mills, High Town, Lancaster LA1 4XS U.K.

First edition.
Printed in Canada.

Legal Deposit—First Quarter
Library of Congress Catalog Card Number: 2022944732
Library and Archives Canada Cataloguing in Publication
Title: Secure parent, secure child : how a parent's adult attachment shapes the
security of the child / Annette Kussin, M.S.W., R.S.W.
Names: Kussin, Annette, author.
Description: "MiroLand imprint, 40."
Identifiers: Canadiana (print) 20220410720 | Canadiana (ebook)
2022041078X | ISBN 9781771837750 (softcover)
ISBN 9781771837767 (EPUB)
Subjects: LCSH: Parenting. | LCSH: Parent and child. | LCSH: Parenting—
Psychological aspects. |LCSH: Attachment behaviour.
Classification: LCC HQ755.8 .K87 2023 | DDC 649/.1—dc23

The point here is that,
without some sort of secure base,
survival is impossible.
—Jeremy Holmes

CONTENTS

Introduction . . . . *ix*

Chapter 1: What is Adult Attachment
and How Does It Affect Parenting?. *1*

Chapter 2: Determining Your Adult Attachment *17*

Chapter 3: The Neurobiology of Parenting *33*

Chapter 4: Adult Attachment and the Effects on Parenting *45*

Chapter 5: Preoccupied Adult Attachment:
Changing Your Parenting *67*

Chapter 6: Dismissing Adult Attachment:
Changing Your Parenting *77*

Chapter 7: Unresolved Adult Attachment:
Changing Your Parenting *93*

Chapter 8: The Value of Being a Secure
or Earned Secure Parent *101*

Chapter 9: Rupture and Repair *113*

Chapter 10: Matching Affect *127*

Chapter 11: Constitutionality and Attachment
(Nature vs Nurture) *137*

Chapter 12: Conclusion *147*

Bibliography *153*

Acknowledgements *159*

About the Author *161*

INTRODUCTION

You may be a parent who has struggled or is struggling with parenting your child or children. Your children may be biological, adopted, or foster children. You may be grandparents who now have custody of your grandchildren. You may be an aunt, an uncle or another relative who has custody of your relative's child. You may be a single parent, a widowed parent, a separated or divorced parent or in a blended family. No matter how you became a parent or your parental situation, parenting is a challenging role. It is more challenging if your children have unresolved issues from being adopted or fostered, having lost a parent, or having experienced other traumatic events. It is more challenging if your children have special needs. It is the most challenging if you have unresolved issues from your own childhood. And almost half of all parents have such issues.

There are many parenting courses that teach strategies on how to effectively parent children. Typically, these courses focus on the behaviour of the children. Some of these include:

Positive Parenting
Parenting your Difficult Child
Parenting after Divorce

Avoiding Power Struggles
Adoption Parenting Classes
Parenting and Technology
Attachment Based Parenting

You may have taken such courses. You may have tried to implement the strategies you learned. You may have had success with some of them. You may still be using the parenting guidelines and approaches or methods you were taught. But I suspect many of you became frustrated that the parenting approaches which you learned were limited in their impact. Your frustration may have resulted because you could not implement the approaches as consistently as needed, or you could not coordinate them with your partners or spouses, or you were too tired and frustrated to apply the approaches. Perhaps your children did not respond well to the methods you applied, or they did not seem relevant to your children and the behaviours they were presenting.

Maybe the parenting methods worked on your younger children but not on your older children and certainly not on your teenage children. You then realized you had to take another course to figure out how to parent your older children.

This book takes a quite different approach to parenting, one that is more challenging than direct parenting approaches. Yet, in the long run, you will be more effective in developing secure and emotionally healthy children. It is based on the Theory of Attachment and is focused on your adult attachment.

The Theory of Attachment proposes that how we are responded to by our parents/caregivers shapes our beliefs about ourselves and our relationships. Whether we perceive ourselves as lovable and worthy of being treated well or unlovable is based on our early experiences with our caregivers, particularly our mothers. These early relationships also influence our perception and expectations of other relationships as we grow and develop. If we have positive and nurturing experiences with our parents/caregivers, we will expect to be treated well by others. If we have negative, rejecting, inconsistent or harmful experiences we will expect similar behaviour from other children and adults. We don't remember the interactions we have with our parents or caregivers as infants and toddlers. But these interactions are stored as beliefs about ourselves in our brains and unconsciously influence our patterns in relationships for life.

Infants and children need their parents/caregivers for their emotional and physical survival so will learn and practice ways to ensure the parent/caregiver is involved. However, if children come to believe their parent/caregiver is not available or harmful they will shut down their needs for the parent/caregiver.

Both children and adults have different categories of attachment. Children who experience loving, nurturing, and predictable environments develop secure attachments. Children who did not, develop one of three insecure attachments. Adults, also have either a secure or autonomous attachment or one of three categories of insecure attachment.

In the 1950s, a psychologist and researcher, Dr. Mary Main, discovered through her research that if one could determine the adult attachment of the mother, through a structured research protocol, one could predict with a high degree of certainty the attachment of the child. This is highly significant for our understanding of how children become secure or insecure. Dr. Main predicted that the attachment of the parent, particularly the mother, will be transferred to the child, unconsciously, through the mother's interactions with her child from infancy onward. Most mothers with a secure adult attachment will develop secure children. Most mothers with an insecure attachment will transfer this to their child, through their parenting of the child.

So, there is clear evidence from research that the type of adult attachment you have will influence how you parent your children and therefore whether you create secure or insecure attachments in your children.[1]

There are parenting approaches that are based on Attachment Theory. These are valuable for creating a caregiving environment that offers the elements of what children need to develop security. However, if you, as a parent, have an insecure adult attachment, creating a secure environment for your child will be exceedingly difficult despite your best efforts. Your best chance of developing happy, healthy, secure, and successful children is to work on yourself, understand your own attachment, change what you can and accept the aspects of your insecure self with kindness and non-judgment.

This book will help you understand what type of adult attachment you have and the strengths and challenges your type of adult attachment will present in your parenting. Some chapters will offer examples of how a parent with a particular insecure adult attachment category may respond to his or her child. Other chapters will offer practical strategies or ways to change some of the parenting practices that result from having an insecure adult attachment. Every parent, both secure and insecure, can benefit from an awareness of their adult attachment and its effect on parenting. Every parent can develop parenting practices that ensure the development of securely attached children.

Having awareness of your adult attachment, whether secure or insecure, will enable you to provide a more secure environment for your child. This awareness will diminish the likelihood that your unconscious beliefs about relationships and your patterns in creating closeness or distance in relationships will be transferred to your child. Your awareness is your first step in changing how you parent.

---

1 Mary Main & Hesse, Erik, "The Adult Attachment Interview," in Cassidy, Jude and Shaver, Phillip, *Handbook of Attachment*, Guilford Press, NY, pg. 406-408.

Chapter 1

WHAT IS ADULT ATTACHMENT AND HOW DOES IT AFFECT PARENTING?

The idea of Adult Attachment was developed by a researcher named Dr. Mary Main. She was a colleague of and fellow researcher with Dr. John Bowlby who developed the theory of attachment. She and another colleague, Dr. Mary Ainsworth, developed the categories of attachment in children. The different experiences that children have with their caregivers create different categories of child attachment.

In the 1950s Dr. Ainsworth and Dr. Main studied young children and the relationship with their mothers. Their observations led to the development of a research protocol for assessing the type of attachment the children had. The research protocol is called the Strange Situation. The protocol looks at how very young children react to being separated from their mothers, how they react to a stranger trying to comfort them and then how they reunite with their mother. They discovered that the children who had a secure relationship with their mother would be upset at being separated from their mother but would be comforted when the mother returned. The secure child could then focus on playing with toys, knowing his/her mother was near by. Other children were upset at being separated from their mothers but were not comforted or settled when reunited. The researchers labeled these children with an Anxious Ambivalent Insecure Attachment. Other children were not upset by the mother leaving and seemed indifferent when the mother returned. These children were classified as having an Avoidant Insecure Attachment. Eventually Dr. Main discovered another category of insecure child. This child did not seem to know what to do when reunited with her/his mother and demonstrated confusing and disorganized behaviour. These children were classified as having a Disorganized Attachment.

These protocols have been tested many times and are now considered established and proven methods of determining the attachment category of the child. The researchers came to understand that children with consistent, loving, and supportive caregivers develop Secure Attachments. Children with inconsistent caregivers develop Anxious/Ambivalent Attachments. Children with rejecting, hostile or unavailable caregivers develop Avoidant Attachments. Children who have abusive or severely neglecting parents are so confused and frightened by their parents that they develop Disorganized Attachments.

These categories are the ones I will use in this book for children's attachment: Secure Attachment, Anxious/Ambivalent Attachment, Avoidant Attachment and Disorganized Attachment.

In time Dr. Main became more interested in the parents of the children in her research and came to believe that it was the parents' patterns of relating that influenced the attachment of the child. She began to study the mothers of the children and in the 1960s developed a means of determining their adult attachment. She created a standardized questionnaire that could determine the category of adult attachment of the parents by trying to access their conscious and unconscious memories and descriptions about their own childhood experiences. Similar to child attachment classifications she determined that adults had four categories of attachment: one secure and three insecure types: Autonomous, Preoccupied, Dismissing and Unresolved.

To help better understand the continuum of child attachment into adult attachment, examine the chart below.[2]

Child Attachments	Adult Attachments
Secure Attachment: Have a parent/caregiver who is consistently available, empathic to their child, gets pleasure interacting with the child, supportive to the child in times of illness or stress. Child trusts parent and turns to them for comfort and support Child has positive self-perception	*Autonomous*: In the Adult Attachment Interview describes a coherent narrative about childhood experiences. Values relationships and turns to intimate others for comfort and security Is self-reflective and accepts that others have different perceptions Is adaptable, open, self-regulated Has a positive and realistic view of self

2 Hesse, "The Adult Attachment Interview," in Cassidy, Jude & Shaver, Phillip, *Handbook of Attachment*, 1999, Guilford Press, New York, chapter 19.

Anxious/Ambivalent:

Have a mother/caregiver who
is inconsistently available
Do not trust caregivers but long
for closeness
Dependent, sensitive to adults
being unavailable and have fear
of abandonment
Have difficulty separating
Manipulative, clingy and
difficulty regulating feelings

Preoccupied:

In the Adult Attachment
Interview describes confusing
childhood experiences with
mother who was inconsistently
available
Is overly dependent on close
relationships
Seeks approval from others
and fears being devalued
Exhibits high levels of emotional
intensity
Impulsive in reactions
Views self as unworthy
and others as superior.

Avoidant:

Have mothers/caregivers who
are unavailable, rejecting,
hostile, indifferent
Learn to deny feelings, needs
and wants
Avoid close relationships
Appear independent and aloof
Believe they have to take care
of themselves
May be caregivers, compliant
and display only positive affect

Dismissing:

In the Adult Attachment Interview describes family history of
rejection or unavailability but
denies importance on their
development
Often idealizes parents
Has difficulty recalling history
Needs to be independent,
self-sufficient
Focuses more on activities
to avoid intimacy
Suppresses feelings and needs
Views self as superior

Disorganized:	*Unresolved:*
Have a caregiver who is abusive or severely neglectful	In the Adult Attachment Interview describes confused and incoherent family history
Conflicted by desire to run to caregiver for support and flee from caregiver who is source of fear	Has not resolved early trauma or loss
Respond with fight, flight or freeze	Perceives relationships as dangerous
No organized way of attaching	May view self as victim
Hypervigilant of abuse or harm	May become aggressor to avoid feeling vulnerable
	May dissociate.
	Displays unpredictable feelings and behaviour

Attachment research informs us that attachment is a continuum. What happened to you in your childhood relationships remains within you, in your brain at an unaware level and continues to influence your relationships for life. The research also reveals that the attachment template you developed will influence the attachment of your children, unconsciously, through your parenting.

How does your child attachment develop into a similar adult attachment?

If you had parents or caregivers who made you feel loved, nurtured, and safe and who were available when you were stressed or scared, you probably learned very early in your childhood that you could trust them. You would believe that you were a lovable human being, worthy of care and love. You would believe that you could express your needs, wants, and feelings to your parents and be responded to with empathy and understanding. You would have a Secure Attachment.

You would feel this security and self-love deep inside you. You would take this good feeling out into the world and other people would respond positively to your ability to be empathic and accepting of others, to your ability to express yourself without overreacting, and to your confidence. As a child this would mean that other children would like you and want to play with you. Teachers would welcome you in their class and encourage you to be a leader. Other parents would want you to be friends with their children. The responses of other people would confirm for you that you were lovable and worthy of good treatment. Your secure attachment would be reinforced in childhood, adolescence, and young adulthood.

If you had a parent or another primary caregiver who was not consistently loving and available to meet your needs, you would feel anxious and angry inside. With such a parent, you could not predict when he or she would be emotionally available to you. Your parent may have been caught up in his or her own emotional needs and focused on other relationships, not you. You would need to watch for the time when your parent/caregiver would be available. You may have learned that, if you were loud and demanding, your parent would pay attention to you. You would end up feeling dependent on your parent, yet not be able to rely on her or him with any consistency. This kind of parent, who is inconsistently available, leaves a child feeling confused, anxious, angry, overly dependent, and hypersensitive to their parent not being available. This type of parent may be overinvolved with their child, for the needs of the parent, not the child.

Such children then go out into the world feeling needy, anxious, and hypersensitive to anyone else not giving them constant attention, such as friends, teachers, or helpers. They become angry and demanding when they do not receive sufficient attention from others. This anger and intense neediness results in alienating other adults and children in their lives. The distancing or rejection from others reinforces the feeling and belief in the child that he or she is not lovable, and that no one is consistently available.

Think about the child who is whiney and demanding in daycare or school. Or the child who acts out and we refer to their behaviour as attention seeking. These children are often labelled as difficult, may be reprimanded for their behaviour, or be sent out of the classroom. Often, teachers do not understand that these children have insecure attachments. These are the children who need a daycare staff or teacher to be consistently available to the child, to bring them close to them and to ensure that they provide extra attention.

As adolescents such insecure children would continue to be dependent, demanding, and dramatic in peer relationships and particularly in romantic relationships. Boyfriends and girlfriends would get tired of such emotional demands and intensity, ambivalent about their commitment and eventually break up with the insecure partner. This would confirm for the adolescent that no one is consistently available in an intimate relationship. Such children and adolescents have Anxious/Ambivalent attachments.

If you had a parent who was rejecting or distant and not able to show love and care, you would also feel insecure. You may have learned to avoid your parents, take care of their needs or become what they wanted and needed you to be. You would have learned to push away your needs, wants and feelings and your own interests or ambitions. Being close to people would be difficult for you. You may deny the value of intimate relationships.

You may have figured out that, if you are the best at what you do, such as being the best student or the best hockey player or the prettiest or most handsome child, your parent would love you, or at least pay attention to you. However, all these successes meet the needs of your parent, not necessarily yours. You would not be able to tell your parent that you are not interested in a particular activity or are worried about your performance. Think about the child who must be the best hockey player and whose parent becomes enraged if he or she is not performing perfectly. Or the children that become fashion models or actors at a very young age, pushed by a parent who needs the success of the child for their own selfish needs. We have witnessed examples of parents who paid for their children to get into expensive and prestigious schools. Such children were not necessarily hard working academically or ambitious but entered such schools because of their parents' interests and needs.

You may have been responsible and well behaved and may have been asked by teachers or others to lead the class or perform other duties. You may have looked independent and even happy, but this would have been based on an insecure foundation. So again, the people around you would treat you well, perceive you as independent, hardworking, responsible, and likeable. They would confirm for you that being strong, independent, and invulnerable was valued. They would not know that you felt lonely and vulnerable inside. You would certainly not feel safe and entitled to go to another adult to share your feelings and worries, vulnerabilities, or fear of failing. Intimacy would be difficult for you. You would develop an Avoidant Attachment.

If you had a parent who was frightening, severely neglecting, or emotionally, physically, or sexually abusive, you would feel very scared and insecure. You may have responded to this fear by being aggressive or avoiding your abusive caregiver or you may have just frozen your feelings and your body, so you would not have to feel anything. Children with such parents see their parents/caregivers as dangerous and certainly cannot turn to them for comfort or support. Such an experience would be very confusing for a child. When a child is frightened, they instinctively turn to the parent for safety, support, and comfort. If the parent is the cause of the child's fear, the child does not know what to do. When such children go out into the world to daycare, schools, and the community, they typically see the world and everyone in it as potentially dangerous and not to be trusted. As adolescents, they may become more aggressive and defiant as protective measures, further alienating others. They may engage in dangerous and harmful behaviours. Other adults often perceive such teens as dangerous, not as confused, traumatized children with Disorganized Attachments.

If you lost a parent when you were very young, to death or abandonment, you would also fear getting close to anyone. If this loss was not resolved, you would continue to believe that depending on anyone is not safe because you can lose this person or may be the cause of their death or abandonment.

Every child needs to feel close to a parent to find love, safety, and comfort and will use different ways to do this. All the behavioural descriptions of the children I just presented are their ways of trying to get close to a parent. Children with inconsistently available parents will try and get close by being demanding and/or manipulative. Children with unavailable parents will try and find some closeness by not demanding too much, taking care of a parent, or being the perfect child. Children with abusive, frightening, or neglectful parents are too confused to have any organized way of getting close. Getting close to their parents may result in being hurt or frightened so they don't know what to do. They may still use strategies to get close, but these are very disorganized and unpredictable.

Every child will internalize the experience of the relationship with his or her caregiver. After many hundreds of interactions with the parent, the child learns what to expect from the parent and comes to believe that they deserve whatever treatment the parent offers. Some children will feel they deserve love and caring while others come to believe they do not. Some will trust the parent to love and care for them and others will not. This feeling and belief about themselves becomes deeply embedded in the brain of the child and continues to operate at an unaware level. This is also true about their expectations of relationships. Whatever relationship children experienced with their parents becomes the template for other relationships. Children that were treated well will expect others to be loving and trustworthy and to treat them well. Children that did not receive unconditional and consistent love from parents will assume all other relationships will be the same. These children will interact in relationships based on such expectations and, as a result, have their beliefs about relationships confirmed. By adulthood, the patterns of relating are deeply entrenched and without an adult's awareness of them, highly resistant to change.

To summarize, your adult attachment develops from your early childhood experiences plus the experiences in childhood from other adults and children and the experiences in adolescence and early adulthood. These later life experiences usually confirm your beliefs about your self-worth and what to expect in relationships. If you are lucky, you may find other people who treat you well and don't confirm your negative self-perception and expectations in relationships. But you would have to be quite lucky.

Here are some examples of clients that I have seen who tried many approaches to help their children. It is only when they learned more about their own adult attachment that they could change how they parented their child or understand their limitations in parenting their child and be less angry at their child and themselves.

Donald was an older single parent of an adopted boy. He was left to raise this child alone after his wife died. His son, Gerald, had many problems. He was aggressive, defiant, had learning difficulties, and did not trust any adult. Donald had taken all the required courses with his wife pre-adoption and thought he was prepared to handle his son. After his wife died, he took more parenting courses and put his son in play therapy. None of these approaches seemed to help his son who became more aggressive and defiant with teachers, with other children and with Donald. Donald was desperate to help his son but did not know what his son needed to become a happier and well-adjusted child.

Jane and Peter were the parents of a teenage girl who had always performed well in school and who had been a problem-free child. As a teenager their daughter started doing poorly in school, became depressed, refused to go to school, stopped seeing her friends and developed obsessive compulsive behaviour. Her parents tried different forms of therapy for their daughter and themselves. They watched their daughter continue to slide into a state of serious depression and anxiety and felt helpless to help her.

Donald and Jane and Peter were all parents who cared deeply for their children. They sought various kinds of parenting courses and therapy in their desperation to help their children with the problems they were presenting. I offer these examples to demonstrate that, without an understanding of attachment theory and specifically your type of adult attachment, you will be limited in understanding and helping your child.

Your adult attachment will be the primary influence on your parenting, more so than the parenting courses you take or the parenting books that you read.

Let me explain with more detail and examples.

If you have a Secure/Autonomous Adult Attachment, you like yourself, trust others, are open with your feelings and open to the feelings and perceptions of others. You tend to be self-aware and probably not judgmental of yourself and of the different views of others. You can express your feelings and needs in a composed regulated way and feel, in a well-adjusted way, that you are entitled to having your feelings heard and your needs met. You are probably in a healthy relationship with a partner/spouse and respect that your partner also has feelings and needs that may be different than yours. You can balance both your feelings and needs and those of your partner/spouse.

Your security as an adult will allow you to be comfortable being a parent. You will be available to your baby consistently enough, able to figure out what his or her cries mean and how to respond. You will be patient with your baby/child when he or she is having a difficult time and comfort your baby/child when he or she is stressed. You will also get pleasure and have fun in the interaction with your baby and young child. You will be able to identify, without judgement, what is difficult for you as a parent and respond appropriately. You will be able to turn to others, particularly your partner or spouse when you are tired or overwhelmed by the needs of your baby or child. But after a break you will find your inner strength and be fully available to your baby or child. Your child will feel that you are able to respond to his/her needs, wants, and feelings and do so balancing empathy and limits.

Because of your adult security and your consistent empathy, nurturing, understanding, and attuned responses to your baby's and child's needs, you will raise a Securely Attached child.

Case example:

Karen was a client who had some issues but had a Secure Adult Attachment. She reported an incident to me that she handled well because of this security. Her young son was very angry at his younger brother and became aggressive with him. Karen was very calm but clear in her response to this. She was empathic in connecting to the angry feelings of her son and reflecting to him that she understood that his younger brother could be annoying. However, she was clear that he could not hit his brother but needed to express his anger verbally and come to her for help. Her son cried and was comforted by his mother.

If you have an insecure adult attachment you are going to fit into one of the three categories of Insecure Attachment. People with an Anxious or Preoccupied Attachment are usually insecure about the availability of others, tend to define their sense of self based on other people, see themselves as inferior to others, are extremely dependent on others, and have poor control of their feelings of anxiety and anger. They tend to be demanding of the attention of others and preoccupied with the whereabouts of a spouse, partner or parent. Because of their own insecurity and constant worry about the availability of others, they are not fully available to their children.

If you are a parent with a Preoccupied Attachment you are going to be inconsistently available to your baby. This is not intentional. Your mind and attention are not fully focused on your baby. Your baby will sense this, so when you are preoccupied with other people, thoughts or worries, your baby will have to be more emphatic in expressing his or her needs. Your baby will cry louder and, if you are still not available, will cry louder and louder, until you have no choice but to focus on your baby. However, you may do this half heartedly and feeling irritable because you have other worries going round and round in your brain. Your baby will not trust you to be consistent in your availability so your baby will have to figure out when you are fully in tune with him or her and continue to watch for such moments. As your baby grows and develops, he or she will use more complex strategies to get your attention. Your child may become louder and louder in his/her demands or become physically aggressive. Your child may become whiney and needy and not able to leave you. Your baby and young child will be hyper-aware watching for your availability. Babies and children should not have to do this.

Example:

I worked with a woman, Elaine, who is the mother of two children. Elaine is insecure, has not been able to achieve her goals in any area of study, blames others for her lack of success, and is constantly in a state of anxiety, anger, and unhappiness. She is inconsistently available to her children and one of her children is very sensitive to this. He is very dependent on his mother, very anxious separating from her, very needy and whiney, and very reluctant to try new and challenging activities. Elaine is inconsistent in her limit setting and depending on her mood is either loving and available or angry and wanting to be left alone. Her son has an Anxious/Ambivalent Attachment because of his mother's Preoccupied Adult Attachment.

You may have another type of insecure adult attachment called Avoidant/ Dismissing. People with a Dismissing Adult Attachment value success and achievement more than intimate relationships. You may find that being busy and active is easier than closeness to others. You may have difficulty being close to your child/ren. You may be involved in their activities and closely follow their school success, but I doubt that your children could express their feelings to you or turn to you when they are vulnerable and upset. You would probably be less interested in your child as an infant except to ensure you are the best parent. This would mean that you make sure your baby is well looked after, is clean, well fed, well dressed, and has a predictable routine. These are all important parenting qualities but not enough for a child to feel loved and understood. You may be a mother or father who would rather be working or being busy than being with your child.

Your baby and young child will sense this and come to believe that they will not get your emotional input unconditionally. Some babies will simply shut down and not express feelings or needs. Others become perfectly behaved and successful children hoping this will please you and bring some closeness with you. Other children may try and take care of your needs hoping this will get your love. Others just give up on getting much involvement from you as a parent and on accomplishing much.

The example of Donald I offered earlier in this chapter is of a parent with a Dismissing Adult Attachment. Donald was unable to express his feelings or be close to his son. He tried to find others to help his son and was committed to providing a stable home for him. He was unable to connect with him emotionally and remained angry at his son for making Donald's life so difficult. His son gradually withdrew from his father, staying in his room, eating meals separately and eventually moving out in his teens. His son also had difficulty trusting other people and became somewhat isolated in his teenage years.

People with a history of trauma or significant loss which remains unresolved have Disorganized or Unresolved Adult Attachment and have the most difficulty being healthy parents. They have a deep fear of closeness, either because closeness is dangerous where you could be harmed or where closeness is untrustworthy because you can lose the one you love. They feel chaotic inside because of this fear so are very disorganized in their responses to their children. They can be loving and kind, angry and rejecting, physically or sexually abusive or severely neglecting. These mood changes and behaviours have little to do with what the child is doing. The child does not know which parent will emerge so are always on guard. These children learn this very early in their development and learn to: placate an abusive parent, avoid them, particularly when they are drinking or drugged, or just freeze and allow whatever abuse is going to happen.

I had a female client who described having an abusive mother with serious mental health problems. Her mother berated my client as a child, neglected her and at times was physically abusive. The father had abandoned the family when the children were young. My client remained very traumatized by her early childhood experiences. She had two children who also had serious problems because my client was so dysregulated and disorganized in her responses to her children and still involved in a very troubled relationship with her own mother.

Your adult attachment will clearly influence how you parent your child. I am sure you want to be the best parent you can be. You had children believing you would be a good parent and certainly better than the parents you had, if they were problematic. However, despite your best intentions, your own inner sense of self, perceptions of relationships, and/or trust or mistrust in others will dominate your ability to offer security, safety and nurturing to your child/ren. To be the best parent you can be, you will need to understand your own adult attachment, understand how it influences your parenting, work through unresolved attachment issues from your past, change what you can, and accept and own what you cannot change. This awareness and non-judgmental acceptance of yourself will enable you to be aware of the feelings, needs, and wants of your child or children and to respond with empathy and understanding. As a secure and aware parent, you will develop secure, aware, and successful children.

Chapter 2

DETERMINING YOUR ADULT ATTACHMENT CATEGORY

⌒

My previous book *It's Attachment, A New Way of Understanding Yourself and Your Relationships*, published by Guernica Editions in 2020, was written to help people determine their attachment categories and change those attachments that are insecure. It's a book for those of you interested in understanding your adult attachment and how it affects adult intimate relationships.

This chapter will help you determine your adult attachment category so you can understand how it affects your parenting rather than your relationships with partners or spouses. To determine your attachment category, you can have a formal Adult Attachment Assessment done by someone trained to do this. This process is costly and there are few therapists trained to conduct and score the structured attachment interview. There are questionnaires that ask questions about how you feel about your partner and how you behave in your couple relationships. These questionnaires reveal your conscious awareness of your feelings and behaviour.

To determine more accurately your adult attachment, you need to become aware of the unconscious aspects of your self, recall your early childhood experiences and figure out how your childhood impacted your adult development. Even without doing a formal assessment it is possible to get an impression and understanding of the different attachment categories and of your attachment type. You will need to examine the description of the different classifications and be honest with yourself about which applies to you.

The following describe the different categories. These include the different ways of parenting or caregiving that you remember experiencing as a young child and the behaviour and attitudes that apply to each attachment category. Read each one carefully and apply whatever descriptions ring true for you. Write them down. You may find that descriptions from more than one category apply to you. Once you have an idea or impression of your adult attachment category, you will be able to understand in later chapters how this influences your parenting.

Secure/Autonomous Attachment

People with Secure/Autonomous Adult Attachments can usually describe their childhood experiences with ease and openness and have many early memories. So, if you had a secure upbringing and were telling this to a friend or someone interviewing you, this is what your story would sound like:

In describing your relationship with your primary caregiver, particularly your mother, you would say that she was loving, available, fun, affectionate and supportive during times of emotional stress or when you were physically hurt or ill.

You would be able to access childhood memories that substantiate the above descriptions. You could describe these memories to someone with enough detail, easy flow, and openness that they sound believable and coherent. You may want to try and do this.

Below are other qualities that Autonomous/Secure Adults have in themselves and/or demonstrate in relationships.

- You value relationships and believe that a close intimate other is important in your life.
- You ensure you have time for relationships and turn to intimate others both when you want to share happy experiences and when you need support and care because you are stressed or sad about events in your life.
- You also are comfortable being independent and on your own. You like yourself, have confidence in your abilities and personal qualities, and enjoy doing some activities on your own.
- You can accept when your spouse, partner or children separate from you and have other important relationships in their lives.
- When you do have problems in relationships, you examine and accept your part in such problems. You can reflect on yourself, accept your mistakes, learn from them, and change your behaviour.
- You believe that you will be able to resolve problems in relationships and do not worry that the relationship is threatened by conflict and will terminate.
- This ability to accept yourself also allows you to be accepting of the differences in others. You can accept that your partner/spouse, parent, or close friend have different perceptions or ideas about issues and different beliefs about parenting.
- You can express your needs, wants, and feelings in relationships in an emotionally balanced way.
- You can be sympathetic, empathic, and understanding of the needs and feelings of others, including your children.
- You can set aside your needs and feelings at times, without resentment, and meet the needs of your partner. You can do this, knowing from experience, that your needs will be met at another time.

- You're a person that others want to have as a friend or partner or parent. You're probably successful in your career, in your parenting and in your close relationships. You usually feel good about yourself. You feel secure.

Earned Security

Earned Security is a concept developed by Mary Main and Associates[3] to explain why some people who describe terrible family histories score as Secure/Autonomous on the Adult Attachment Interview or present as secure in relationships as described by the above descriptions. This category is very hopeful for those individuals who were raised in an insecure parenting environment. They can achieve secure adult attachments. How does one overcome such detriments and develop into a secure adult? This can occur for several reasons.

A child may have alternative attachment figures in his or her life. This can be the parent of a friend whom the child sees often and who treats the child in a caring and loving manner. It can be a teacher who may know about a child's difficult home life and offer them much support and nurturing. Teachers see children daily for at least a school term so they can play the role of an attachment figure. A child may have a relative, like a grandparent or aunt or uncle, who is loving and caring and whom the child sees often. Alternative attachment figures must see a child with enough intensity and frequency to influence a child's attachment. Children will take in positive experiences with another adult and come to believe that they are lovable and worthy only if they spend lots of time with that adult.

---

3 Hesse, Erik, "The Adult Attachment Interview," in Cassidy, Jude & Shaver, Phillip, *Handbook of Attachment*, 1999, Guilford Press, New York, p.401

An adolescent may come to recognize that their parent or parents are not consistently caring adults, not available much of the time, or abusive and neglectful. Because the adolescent brain is rapidly changing, particularly the thinking and analyzing section of the brain, adolescents have a greater capacity to think about their family situation. Because peers become more important as attachment figures, the adolescent may seek out peers that are supportive. A boyfriend or girlfriend may understand the background of the adolescent they are dating or partnered with and remain in the relationship during difficult times. An adolescent may experience a friend or the parents of a friend as caring and empathic. He or she may come to believe that other people are not like their parents and come to trust close relationships.

An adult may also choose a partner or spouse who offers him or her a nurturing unconditional loving experience that changes his or her negative belief about relationships and perception of themself. This may occur because of luck, circumstances or because one is determined not to partner with or marry someone like his or her parent.

A child, adolescent, or adult may enter therapy and develop a relationship with a therapist that is caring, nurturing, and supportive. In time this relationship changes the old negative self-perception and mistrust of relationships to one that is positive, involving trust and security in relationships. Adolescents and adults are most able to use a therapeutic relationship to examine their early childhood experiences, come to understand the impact on their personalities, begin to risk being more open and trusting in the therapeutic relationship, and eventually transfer this to the relationships in their lives.

Typically, people with Earned Security have come to understand that their childhood experiences created significant setbacks for them in relationships but also positive attributes and successes. They understand why their parents parented them so poorly and may have forgiven them. They've used this insight to make changes in their own patterns in relationships and come to perceive themselves as valuable and worthy of caring and success in their lives. Thus, they have earned their security. If you have put yourself in this category, you will be a secure parent, generally, but may have some vulnerable times with your children when you overreact or feel the need to withdraw. You will be able to think about your reaction, calm yourself, and urge yourself to be emotionally available. If you need to withdraw, you will come back to your children with a reassuring and loving response.

Example:

I will use myself as an example of this category. I was an Avoidant Child and Dismissing Young Adult. I had great difficulty getting close to people and making commitments in relationships with boyfriends. I was very successful in my profession and pursuits but not in close relationships. I did not express vulnerable feelings or turn to others for support and nurturing. Through therapy and other healthy relationships, I was able to understand my childhood, work through some difficult early experiences, work hard at changing, and eventually came to feel secure and emotionally aware and available. I developed the category Earned Secure Adult Attachment.

I remember a time when my daughter was a young child, and I was annoyed at her. I did not express my anger but rather I became controlling, demanding, and punitive. My daughter said: "You sound just like baba." Baba was my mother who had been a distant and emotionally unavailable mother because of her difficult childhood. My mother had been angry at me for not being the daughter she longed for and could be critical and controlling. I was shocked to hear these words from my daughter. I had worked very hard not to parent how my mother parented. However, my daughter was correct, and I had to stop and reflect on how I was parenting in that moment. I was able to hear my daughter's reflection of me, apologize to her, and we were able to talk and resolve the issues between us. I was able to do this because of my Earned Security.

Preoccupied-Anxious Attachments

To determine if you fit into this category, check to see if the following descriptions apply to you.

If you were describing your family history to a therapist, it would be in a confusing and rambling manner. You would describe your mother or primary caregiver as sometimes wonderful and involved with you and sometimes angry and rejecting of you. You would describe not being able to predict which mood she would have and so you were always checking on this. You might describe feeling anxious and angry at your mother.

You may also describe your mother or primary caregiver as overinvolved with you and anxious about any independence you expressed. Your parent would need you to be available to her or him and would be overinvolved with your school, friends, and activities.

As an adult you still have this feeling of anxiety and insecurity. You feel a desperate need for relationships and are dependent on others for your security and self-worth.

- Because of the inconsistent availability of your parent or their overinvolvement, you are very vigilant about the availability of any partner and are easily triggered into feelings of jealousy and insecurity. You think about your partner/spouse a great deal of your time, particularly when you are away from him or her. These insecure feelings may lead you to accuse your partner/spouse of having affairs or caring about their colleagues and other people more than you. You may start to check on their whereabouts or check their emails and messages. This desperate and demanding behaviour may push away the person or people you care about. Even knowing this, often does not help you stop your behaviour.

- You have great difficulty controlling your feelings. Whether you are feeling anger, sadness, fear, anxiety, or joy you experience these feelings with great intensity. You may have learned in childhood that, if you expressed your needs with intensity, such as having temper tantrums, your parent would pay attention to you. You may continue to believe this but now you are an adult and expressing your feelings with great force usually pushes people away. Certainly, it does not bring them closer.

- You have difficulty parenting. You may experience your children as too demanding and find yourself getting angry at them. You may have difficulty allowing your children to be independent and find yourself being threatened by relationships that they have with other adults and even other children. Yet at other times you wish your children would leave you alone and go off with other people so that you can focus on your own worries or spend your time talking to other adults.

- You have great difficulty being independent, making independent decisions, and trusting your judgment. You rely on others to direct you but may need the opinions of many others, which in the end is confusing and leaves you helpless to make any decision. This inability to make your own decisions applies to your parenting. You need to ask your partner or spouse or your parents or friends—or anyone who will listen—what to do about your children.

- You tend to overvalue your partner or spouse, particularly in the beginning of a relationship and devalue yourself. You do not understand why the person has chosen you; yet you become involved very quickly. Your intense feelings and immediate dependency may drive the person away.

Case Example:

Sonia came to me as an older woman, in her sixties, who was having great difficulty in her long-term marriage. The husband she had ideal-ized was no longer behaving wonderfully and she was struggling with what to do about her marriage. She was angry at her husband and anxious about his lack of interest in her. But she remained completely dependent on him. Sonia described her early childhood as wonderful but acknowledged that she was always with her parents and that they never encouraged her to be independent. She was very close to her mother who could be very loving, but also angry and demanding. Her parents had experienced severe trauma in their lives and so felt the need to be overprotective of their daughter.

When Sonia met Peter, the man who would become her husband, she fell head over heels in love. She thought he was perfect. He was outgo-ing, charming, successful, and had many friends. Sonia was shy, more bookish, and had very few friends. She became totally preoccupied with Peter, secretly following him.

Eventually, Peter asked Sonia to marry him. Her parents were not thrilled with Peter. He wasn't of their faith and culture, but Peter assured Sonia's father that he would take care of her and provide a good life for her. Sonia married Peter, believing she'd found the perfect man. She entered his world, became part of his social life, took on his interests, and helped him in his business. She helped create the image of a perfect family life, where her husband and children looked good, where the house in which they lived was spectacular and where she made her husband feel that whatever he took on he did flawlessly. Sonia's sense of self was completely tied to the lifestyle and personal-ity of her husband. When her mother died, Sonia needed her husband more and soon became more aware of his unavailability. She began noticing his attentiveness to others and his preference for his activities over her. She began to feel anger and expressed this with intense feelings and actions, until on one day she became enraged and threw something at her husband in front of their friends.

When Sonia had children, her husband was not very available, so she relied on her mother to help with her parenting. She would leave her children if her husband asked her to go with him on a trip even if this was not in the best interest of her children. When her children were older, they were angry with her, feeling she was too needy and demanding of them.

The relationship with her husband deteriorated but Sonia couldn't let go of Peter because she continued to idealize him. She remained preoccupied with him long after the marriage ended. With the end of the marriage, she became more demanding of her children. She felt entitled to demand their time and attention and could not accept they had separate lives that did not include her.

Dismissing/Avoidant Attachments

To determine if you fit into the category of Dismissing Attachment, check to see if the following descriptions apply to you.

- You describe a childhood history of neglect or rejection or conditional love but deny the importance of this on your personality development. For instance, you may say things like: "That happened a long time ago and has nothing to do with my life now."
- You may idealize your parents but cannot give any memories or examples of what they did that validates the idealized adjectives. For example, you may say your mother was a great mother but cannot describe in any detail what she did that was loving or nurturing.

- You may not be able to give any description or a very sparse description of your parents or your early childhood experience saying you do not remember.
- You value your independence and prefer to be self-sufficient and self-reliant. It is difficult for you to ask for help or turn to others for support if you do allow yourself to feel vulnerable.
- You tend to suppress feelings of vulnerability, sadness, or fear. You may allow feelings of anger but rarely recognize that underlying the anger is pain from unmet needs.
- Your needs go unmet because it is so difficult for you to express your needs in close relationships. Expressing needs can make you feel dependent, and this is too frightening for you.
- You prefer to be involved in activities than in close relationships. You may be a workaholic, involved in sports and other extracurricular activities, and prefer to do activities with people rather than talk and share feelings.
- You ensure that you keep your distance from people that you suspect may reject you or whom you consider superior to you.
- You may view yourself as superior or present this image to others.
- You may be very successful in your career, in your chosen activities, or in superficial relationships but find your partner, spouse, girlfriend/boyfriends complaining you are emotionally distant.
- You may be good at doing the practical parenting for your children such as making good lunches or meals, ensuring they are properly dressed and looking good, taking them to their activities, and making sure they do their homework. You may encourage their performance at school, in sports, in the arts or whatever activities you chose for them. You may even expect or demand your children excel at what they do or be perfect.
- You are not as good at being emotionally available to your children, listening to their concerns or fears, or nurturing and comforting them when they are struggling. In fact, your children may not turn to you for comfort and support knowing that you are not available emotionally.

Case Example:

Raymond, in his late 30ties, was a client I had who would fit the description of a Dismissing Attached Adult. He came to see me because he was feeling detached from his wife and generally wasn't in touch with feelings. When I asked him to describe his relationship with his mother, he said she was a housewife. He could not elaborate or give me any other description. He described his father as never home and not involved with his children. His parents seemed very uninvolved with their son.

He described being in love with a girlfriend in university. He had no need to see her frequently nor did he miss her when she attended another university. He would visit her on occasion and felt his limited contact was indicative of his commitment to her. He was shocked when she terminated the relationship telling him that she felt rejected by him and didn't feel he loved her. He missed her after the relationship ended but didn't make any effort to tell her or reconcile with her.

Raymond was very successful in his career and very active in sports. He didn't look forward to going home to his wife and felt no emotional connection to her. He had moved far away from his parents and had very little contact with them. He didn't have any close friends.

Raymond clearly would be categorized as a Dismissing Adult Attachment. He appeared well functioning, was successful in his career and devoted much of his extra time to sports and superficial social activities. He avoided close relationships all his adult life, was out of touch with his feelings and didn't feel any intimacy with his wife. When Raymond had a daughter, he did not feel much for her as an infant and was not involved in her care. As a toddler, his daughter was excited to see him when he returned home and offered her father unconditional love. In time, he began to feel a special love for his daughter and looked forward to coming home to her, not his wife. His daughter's unconditional acceptance of him when she was a young child was the first time Raymond experienced absolute love.

Unresolved/Disorganized Attachments

As I mentioned earlier, people with Unresolved Attachments have usually suffered some trauma or significant loss in their lives which remains unresolved and affects the present. People with Unresolved Attachments demonstrate the following patterns:

- You may describe a confusing and disorganized childhood history, sometimes speaking in the past, sometimes talking as if the past was still present, and sometimes avoiding talking about your history because it is too painful to remember. You may not remember much of your early childhood history if you suffered significant trauma.

- You are easily triggered by many events, situations, and sensory stimulants like taste, touch, smell, and sounds. Being triggered means you react to a situation, person, event, or sensory stimulant in an extreme way that is not appropriate to what happened or what you experienced. This experience can be an emotional one or a sensory one, involving smell, sight, touch, sound, or taste.

- You may find yourself becoming disoriented during difficult discussions or situations and not sure what is happening to you.

- You may disconnect emotionally and psychologically so you feel you are not present in the moment and not relating to the people in your life.

- You may find that you cannot control your emotions and moods and find that your moods change without apparent cause or warning.

- Such changes in moods may be frightening to your children or your spouse/partner, yet you cannot control them.

- You may be unable to sleep well at night because of the intrusion of memories of the trauma, or disturbing thoughts, or because you have troubling dreams or nightmares.
- You cannot concentrate because of intrusive thoughts and memories.
- Sexual intimacy may be difficult for you because of the reminders of earlier sexual abuse.
- In extreme cases a person may not remember what they did or where they were for a day or sometimes days.
- In very extreme and rare cases a person may feel he or she has more than one personality which emerges at different times.

You have difficulty parenting because of your unstable and fluctuating moods and because, at times, the needs and wants of your children trigger you into anger, withdrawal, or fear. You may not understand why you react this way and feel guilty.

Case Example:

Sandra was a client of mine who had experienced sexual abuse as a young child from a nonfamily member. She had tried to repress this experience and focus on being a successful adult. She did achieve some success in her career but had difficulty in her intimate relationship with her husband. She would easily get enraged at him if he complimented her or encouraged her in her activities. In her rage she would explode, throw things, and eventually run from her home. She continued this frightening behaviour after she had children and seemed unable in this state of rage to recognize how harmful this was to her children.

You may discover that more than one description applies to your personality or behaviour. As I mentioned, usually a person has one primary attachment category but may have one or two subcategories.

An example of this is Carrie, a client I worked with who had a mother that was inconsistently available, so as a child my client described feeling anxious and angry at her mother. At times Carrie would be defiant and non-compliant but then would feel that her mother was becoming very distant. This distance would scare Carrie, so she'd find ways to pull her mother back into a closer relationship. She'd become sweet and well-behaved, doing everything to please her mother. Carrie had a grandmother who lived nearby and who was loving and nurturing. Carrie described always trusting that she could go to her grandmother when her mother was angry and rejecting.

Carrie had great difficulty trusting her partner and was very sensitive to his unavailability. If he worked late or was involved with other people, she'd become very jealous and angry. She'd check his phone and emails convinced he was involved with another woman. She would become preoccupied with this, thinking repeatedly that he didn't love her and was seeing someone else. She'd confront him with her suspicions, with intense emotions. She'd become angry, cry, and then beg for reassurance. This aspect of her personality and her emotional behaviour reflected her Preoccupied Attached state of mind.

Carrie could also be reassured by her partner that he loved her and was committed to her. With this reassurance she could calm down, believe her partner's words, could self-reflect and reason with herself that her intense reaction was her insecurity. In her calmer state she had a realistic perception of her partner and knew he was a reliable and trustworthy man. This aspect of herself emerged from her sense of security and autonomy internalized from the relationship with her grandmother.

Carrie displayed both behaviours with her daughter as well. Her daughter had mental health issues and at times Carrie was sensitive to her daughter, able to be empathic, and parent her securely and safely. At other times Carrie withdrew from her daughter, could not connect emotionally with her, and knew she was not meeting the needs of her daughter. Her daughter eventually was placed in a residential treatment setting. Carrie remained committed to working with her daughter and on herself, to become a more secure adult who could be consistent in her attuned parenting of her daughter. In time she was able to do this.

I hope by the end of this chapter you have an impression of your adult attachment category or categories. If you have determined that you have an insecure adult attachment, I hope you will be able to accept this without feeling discouraged or badly about yourself. You developed your adult attachment because of your early history with your caregivers. It was not your fault. Nor the fault of your parents, who probably also had difficult early childhood experiences.

In the later chapters of this book, I will help you understand both, the challenges you will have as a parent based on your adult attachment and, how you can change your parenting behaviour.

Chapter 3

THE NEUROBIOLOGY OF PARENTING

*s a parent, you are going to have a crucial influence on the development of your child's brain. Whether your baby develops self-regulation, and an integrated and optimally functioning brain, will be based on a combination of genetics and the environment you create for your baby and child.

There is evidence that shows that self-regulation, or emotional balance, in children is a predictor of their success academically, socially, and personally. As a parent, understanding how self-regulation develops is important since you will be a significant factor in your child's capacity to be aware of emotions and express them in a balanced and reasonable manner.

Before birth, all the biological needs of the foetus are met by the mother through the umbilical cord. The foetus does not have to communicate its needs. The mother must ensure she takes care of herself, minimizes her stress, and provides the proper nutrition to both her and her developing foetus. All the foetus growing inside the womb needs, to be born a healthy infant, is the mother nurturing herself and normal genetic markers.

At birth the infant enters the world feeling cold, wet, and probably hungry. The infant also arrives with trillions of brain cells unconnected. These cells immediately begin to connect through electrical and chemical stimulants, called transmitters. Think of your brain as a computer connecting with billions of people in cyberspace to both communicate and receive information. The brain is making these connections, driven by both its genetic potential and by its environment. The brain makes these connections most efficiently and productively in a safe predictable environment. The cells that are connected allow for the development of motor skills, language, knowledge, artistic and athletic talents, as well as many other talents and interpersonal connections. The cells that are not used or connected are deleted or pruned. This means that an infant living in a safe predictable and stimulating environment with either biological or other loving caregivers has a greater chance of developing a highly integrated and optimally performing brain than an infant living in a non-nurturing, disorganized, and neglectful environment.

For example, young children raised in a family where they are exposed to different languages will have strong cellular development in the part of the brain where language develops. They will find learning languages easier than a child not exposed to alternative languages. An infant exposed to books and stimulating toys will be more prepared for academic learning. A parent/caregiver who encourages their child to take music lessons or engage in sports at a young age also will promote the connections of the cells related to these potential skills. A child raised without these opportunities will lose the cells. The brain operates from the premise of "use it or lose it" Cells that are used remain connected. Those that are not, are deleted.

As I have stated previously, self-regulation is essential for the overall success of the child. So, how does this develop?

After birth, the infant immediately begins to communicate its needs, typically by crying. The infant's needs may be primitive but are essential for his/her survival. Infants need to be fed, put to sleep, have their diapers changed, and generally have a calm and hygienic environment. They also need love and nurturing on a consistent basis to survive and thrive emotionally.

The physiological needs of the infant activate stress chemicals in the brain. The main stress chemical is called cortisol. If a baby is hungry, they will instinctively feel stressed by this need. The feeling of stress drives the baby to communicate its need and the baby will cry. In this state of tension, the stress chemicals remain activated until the baby's needs for satisfaction and comfort from being fed are realized. Once this need is met, the stress chemicals are reduced, allowing chemicals for pleasure and calm, such as serotonin, to be activated. Serotonin is known as "the happy chemical". It provides feelings of happiness, positivity, and well being. This process of activation and deactivation of stress, allowing peacefulness or calm, is essential for the brain's future functioning and capacity to manage stress.

The production of the chemicals for both stress and for relaxation occur at critical times in the infant's neurological development, usually in the first six months. This means that if the baby's needs, and communication of these needs, are not responded to by the caregiver, the baby may not develop the chemicals and neurological pathways that facilitate the baby's ability to reduce its stress and return to a calm state.

In infancy, it is the mother/caregiver who enables the brain to reduce the stress. This is done by meeting the needs of the infant or addressing the cause that is generating the stress. The onus is on the caregiver to determine what the need or cause is and to alleviate it. The caregiver is the regulator of the stress chemicals in early infancy.

Every mother/caregiver needs to take the time to understand the baby's signals. Some babies are easily comforted, while others are more challenging. A mother or caregiver may believe that he or she has their infant figured out but then the needs of the infant change. It may not be easy to figure out your infant's signals, but a secure attuned mother will listen, observe, and in time come to know her infant. An attuned caregiver is one who understands their baby's internal world and is empathic to the feelings, needs, and wants of the infant. This is both an instinctive and learned response. A secure caregiver will instinctively be tuned into her infant's communications, then take the time to learn the subtleties of these sounds and gestures and respond appropriately.

To quote a well-known neurologist, Allan Schore, who has researched the development of the infant brain:

> *"The vast majority of the development of axons, dendrites and synaptic connections that underlie all behaviour is known to take place in early and late human infancy ... The fact that this growth occurs during the period of close mother-infant interaction suggest both that the organism's post natal environment acts as regulator of brain development and that post natal stages of brain development may provide the explanation for how early experience affects later behaviour."*[4]

I recall a time when I was driving on the highway and my daughter, who was a few months old at the time, started crying. I could not attend to her immediately as I was driving. She started crying louder. I was not able to exit the highway so had to continue driving for some time before I could soothe her. At that point she was screaming. I was in a panic, feeling helpless to do anything. I tried comforting her with

---

4   Alan N. Schore, *Affect Regulation and the Origin of the Self*, 1994, Lawrence Erlbaum Assoc. Inc. Hillsdale, NJ, pg 12.

my voice assuring her that I would be with her shortly, to no avail. I don't know who was more stressed, her or me. When I finally was able to exit the highway and find a safe place to park, she and I were both emotional wrecks. Her diaper was soaking wet. I was able to change the diaper but had to hold her in my arms for quite some time, talking in a soothing voice before she calmed down and fell asleep. I was a wreck for much longer.

Observing and interacting with my granddaughter has confirmed for me all these theories of a child's dependency on a caregiver and the co-regulation that occurs in the early weeks/months of a baby's life. *I watched* my granddaughter be born and was an active participant in the first few months of her life. From early on, I became aware of her signals to indicate what she needed. My daughter, son-in-law, and I watched, listened, and learned the meaning of her signals to communicate. This was not easy and took time. We also experienced our own pain at listening to my granddaughter's cries from the pain of gas. We learned that the one method of soothing her was to hold her and bounce her on a large exercise ball. We did this for hours each day. She was completely dependent on our bouncing and soothing her. She could not do this for herself. The realization of her total dependency on her caregivers for her survival and comfort was profound for me.

Babies offer us many opportunities to know that they need us to pay attention and respond to their needs and wants. However, babies will shut down when they come to believe the caregiver is not available, will reject them, or be punitive and hurtful. A baby that comes to believe the caregiver will not look after him or her will stop communicating their needs. In time that baby may not even be in touch with its feelings of hunger, or the feel of a dirty diaper against its skin, or its need to be touched and held. This is what happened to the babies and children who were adopted many years ago from the orphanages in Romania and other orphanages around the world and continues to happen to this day in impoverished, understaffed, and neglectful orphanages. Such babies can appear to be autistic or cognitively impaired, but they are uncommunicative, unresponsive, and autistic-like because of the trauma from their severe neglect and abuse.

Years ago, I had a case where the parents were adopting their second child from a country in Europe. I had helped them with their first adopted child. They contacted me from this country, very concerned that the child they were planning to adopt was not responding to them. They were sure the child was autistic and did not want to adopt a special needs child. They sent me a video of the child who was 18 months old at the time. This child was non-responsive to them and appeared to be emotionless and unaware of its surroundings. The parents wanted my opinion on whether this child could be autistic. I had to make an assessment from thousands of miles away. I was aware of adopted children who appeared to be autistic, due to the consistent institutional neglect they experienced. These children eventually shut down because no caregiver responded to their signals for closeness and nurture. They became "Institutionally Autistic".

I recommended to my clients that they insist that the orphanage allow them to observe the child interacting with the woman who was his primary caregiver in the orphanage. I knew that orphanages from this country were reluctant to do this. They all had rigid protocols for overseas adoptions. I told these parents to demand this or refuse to adopt the child. The orphanage reluctantly allowed them to observe the interaction between this caregiver and the child. They were able to observe their prospective son smiling and playing with the caregiver. They were deeply relieved and with my ongoing support, adopted this boy, whom we will call Dimitri.

After an initial period of avoiding his parents and remaining unemotional and unresponsive, Dimitri became more trustful of his adoptive mother and eventually developed into a happy expressive child. These parents understood how mistrustful their adopted son was of closeness and were able to remain patient and loving during his long period of rejecting and withdrawing from them. Their consistent calm, empathic, and nurturing response to Dimitri enabled him, gradually, to get in touch with his needs, wants, and feelings and communicate them to his mother and father. Once he communicated these and was able to experience the consistent love, care, and understanding from his parents, he came to believe that caregivers and other adults could be trusted, and he allowed himself to be close and vulnerable with his parents.

In time, a toddler will develop its own capacity to self-regulate, integrating the emotional and rational components of the brain. The toddler will also be able to communicate its needs verbally to a caregiver. The child will be aware of its feelings of stress and will have the capacity to reduce the stress by self soothing methods or turning to an available parent/caregiver. The older child will be able to pause and think about why they are experiencing certain stressful feelings and either turn to adults for support or find her or his own solutions. The three components of the brain will be integrated so the older child will be aware of its feelings, think about what is causing these feelings before reacting, and respond in an appropriate manner.

The responses of the mothers/parents/caregivers to the needs, wants and feelings of their child or children will be determined by their adult attachment. Let me elaborate.

Caregivers with Secure or Autonomous Adult Attachment have the instinct to respond to their baby with what is called *attunement*. As I mentioned previously in the book, attunement is the capacity to read accurately and resonate with what your baby is experiencing inside him or herself. The attuned mother will recognize that one cry means her baby is tired and, if she allows her baby to cry a couple more seconds, he or she will fall asleep. Another cry will mean her baby is hungry and it is time to breast feed or heat up the bottle. A more stressful cry will tell the attuned mother/caregiver that something is bothering her baby and he or she will check the diaper and check other things that could be bothering her baby such as teething. The mother/caregiver will realize her baby may be gassy, ill, colicky or in pain. The attuned caregiver will remain calm and soothing while exploring these sources of her or his baby's cries.

It takes time to recognize the meaning of the different cries and gestures so no caregiver will know this immediately.

In my last book I mentioned a time when my daughter was a few months old and crying unrelentingly. I tried all the methods I knew to soothe her and was growing helpless and stressed when I could not figure out what was bothering her. I was able to get some relief from my husband but both of us were worried. I eventually took her to our family doctor. She could not find anything wrong medically and assured me it was probably a phase of colic caused by gas. She urged me to try different movements to ease the pain in her stomach. I eventually found that bending my knees in an up and down motion, basically hundreds of squats, was the only movement that brought her comfort. I did this for hours. My best friend would come over to assist me and would move up and down holding my daughter. My husband would take over after work. All three of us developed strong legs and my daughter, in time, matured out of this painful phase.

I was able to figure out what worked in easing my daughter's colic because I was secure enough not to personalize her stressful cries, to remain calm while trying different methods to soothe her and to seek help from others when I was too upset or too tired to be helpful to my daughter.

This was also the case with my granddaughter, which I mentioned earlier. My daughter, son in law, and I all took turns bouncing on the exercise ball to soothe her.

Caregivers with insecure adult attachments may lack the capacity for attunement and not be able to respond to their infant with sensitivity and empathy. Because the child's instinctive needs for survival are paramount, the infant/child will in time figure out how best to engage the caregiver, avoid the caregiver, or shut down any needs and feelings. I will elaborate on this more in the following chapters but will explain how the brain adapts to the relationship with the caregiver, developing either good self-regulation, dysregulation, or overregulation.

As I have stated, babies are dependent on their mother/caregiver for their survival. This means that babies may need to figure out how to ensure the caregiver is available. The baby with a secure mother comes to believe that my mother is available on a timely and sensitive basis. This baby trusts that all I must do is communicate my need in a reasonable voice or gesture and my mother responds and knows what I need and want.

If the baby's mother/caregiver is not reliable, is untrustworthy, and does not respond accurately and in a timely manner, the baby will communicate its needs and wants more loudly and demandingly. As these cries increase in intensity and volume, the mother/caregiver eventually will respond but possibly with annoyance or frustration. This would be typical of an insecure preoccupied attached mother/caregiver whose own needs are more paramount at times and because she/he is often preoccupied with other adults who are not available to them. The baby of such mothers/caregivers learns that he or she must communicate needs with emotional intensity and cannot trust its mother/caregiver to be consistently available. The infant remains in an emotionally heightened state.

Other babies learn that, no matter how loud and forcefully they communicate their needs, a caregiver is not available or the caregiver responds with hostility and rejection. Such babies learn to repress their needs since no one is available to take care of them. They may stop crying or reaching out to a caregiver. They may look calm and unstressed, but this is based on their experience that there is no point in expressing their needs. These infants deactivated their needs and wants, leaving their brains out of touch with feelings and needs.

In extreme cases, such as infants from orphanages, infants stop growing and developing although they remain alive. Such infants may learn to self-stimulate since no adult is available to play with them and take an interest in them. They may rock themselves, bang their heads against the crib, stare at their hands, or develop other ways to stimulate or soothe themselves. They stop relying on caregivers to soothe, comfort or stimulate them. Many parents with adopted children have witnessed their infants and toddlers using such harmful self-soothing methods.

Some caregivers will offer a bottle, change a diaper, or put the infant to sleep, but without the warmth, affection, and soothing that the infant also needs. They can do the executive tasks of caregiving but, without expressing love, affection, and understanding. Their infants look well taken care of, are dressed well, and are fed but lack the special emotional connection to the parent. Or if such parents cannot soothe their stressed infant, their own feelings of inadequacy are generated, and they may become angry and withdrawn from their infant. Such caregivers often have Dismissing Adult Attachments.

Parents with Unresolved Adult Attachments are the most harmful to the baby's developing brain. The baby cannot figure out what is the best strategy to get its needs met from the mother/caregiver. There is no consistent pattern in the response from the caregiver. Sometimes the caregiver is attuned and available, sometimes the caregiver is not accessible, and other times the caregiver is scary, angry and may cause the baby physical pain. The baby's brain chemistry remains in an agitated stressed state and its ways of getting the caregiver involved are also unorganized. Sometimes the baby is demanding and may hit the caregiver, sometimes the baby turns away from the caregiver, and sometimes the baby seems totally unresponsive, in a frozen state.

If you placed yourself in one of the insecure adult attachment categories, your baby or child will either be dysregulated, expressing emotions with impulsivity and intensity, or will be overregulated, with repressed affect. You can change your baby's or child's expression of affect by working on yourself and your own regulation of feelings. You can also help your child feel safe in the relationship with you so they can express whatever they are feeling with appropriate regulation. The part of the brain that controls affective expression, the Limbic System, remains flexible for life and amenable to change with consistent and sensitive input. You can change your baby's brain by changing or modifying your adult attachment.

"How we have come to experience the world, relate to others and find meaning in life are based upon how we have come to regulate our emotions."[5]

---

5 Seigel, Daniel J, *The Developing Mind*, 1999, Guilford Press, New York, p.245.

Chapter 4

ADULT ATTACHMENT AND THE EFFECTS ON PARENTING

$\mathcal{O}\!\mathcal{D}$

Every category of adult attachment will present different challenges to parenting. Understanding your primary attachment classification and the challenges you face will help you be a more effective and grounded parent.

Secure/Autonomous Adult Attachment

Generally, people with Secure Autonomous Attachments will have an easier time parenting because their security will allow them:

- to value the relationship with their children even during difficult phases
- to be empathic to their children
- to get pleasure in the interactions with their children
- not to personalize their children's challenging behaviour
- to put aside their needs and wants and focus on the needs of their children
- to offer support and guidance consistently

Parents with Secure/Autonomous Attachments will have challenges with their children but will be able to manage them more calmly and rationally and be able to turn to others for support and guidance. They will be more resilient when they are struggling with a child who has special needs or a child going through a difficult time. They may be exhausted and angry but will bounce back from a taxing period and not blame their child or themselves for being an imperfect parent.

Secure people have a realistic awareness of the challenges of parenting and are both reflective, owning their part in child/parent problems, and kind to themselves when they make mistakes in their parenting role.

Preoccupied Adult Attachments

Let's review the description of the personality and behaviour of a Preoccupied Attached person. And remember, these descriptions are not meant to be criticisms. You developed these beliefs and behaviours as a child to ensure your own needs for closeness, care, and safety were met:

- You are very dependent on other people for your sense of self.
- You do not like being alone and feel anxious and sometimes empty inside when you are alone.
- You will desperately reach out to people rather than be on your own or do an activity on your own.
- You will become attached to people very quickly, even when the other person does not seem as interested or when you have just come to know someone.
- You will be upset if the other person stops showing interest, even pestering that person to stay involved.
- You have a difficult time controlling your feelings, finding yourself becoming angry if someone does not show enough interest in you or is not available when you need them
- You have difficulty making independent decisions, needing the advice of many people.

- You are hypersensitive to other people not being available and may misread their behaviour or not believe their reasons for not calling you, being late, or having to cancel a meeting or social engagement.
- You become preoccupied with the people who have disappointed you, have not been available, or who have ended a relationship with you. Your thoughts about them go round and round in your brain without you being able to control them or deflect from them. As you think about these people your anger increases and you may feel the need to hurt them or find some revenge for their hurting you.
- You may be very conflicted in your close relationships because, on the one hand, you are so dependent on your partner, spouse, best friend, or parent and, on the other, you are so mistrustful and fearful they will reject you, not be available, and not need you.
- You tend to idealize your partner or spouse and put yourself down which leaves you feeling unworthy and bad about yourself.

The strengths you will have as a parent are:

- You can express feelings and show warmth and affection.
- You can be fun and be emotionally available at times.
- You value the relationships with your children even in your inconsistency.
- You may be involved in your children's school and activities.

All these positive qualities are the reasons your children long to be with you and enjoy your company when you are available to them.

The challenges for you in your parenting will be:

- You may be inconsistent in your availability to your children because you are worried and thinking about other relationships and at times give preference to your needs over the needs of your children. For instance, if your husband or partner has not arrived home when they said they would, you will become preoccupied with where they are, why they did not call, and even suspect that they are with another person. In this preoccupied state you may have a hard time staying present for your children. You may ignore your children even though they are asking for your help with something or just want to spend time with you.

- If you are feeling deprived because your spouse/partner is not available or you're a single parent, you may crave adult attention, and be contacting friends, your parents or other people or having people to your home when your children are there. If your children need you and demand your attention you may be unable to focus on them because your own needs are so pressing. You may ignore them, get angry with them, reject them, and tell them to occupy themselves.

- In your preoccupied state, the needs and demands of your children may become annoying and you may become angrier and angrier at them. You may yell at them, punish them, or continue to ignore them.

- You may be overinvolved with your children and have difficulty allowing them autonomy and freedom to develop independent activities and other relationships. You may need to hover over them, ensure that they involve you in most aspects of their life, and communicate frequently with you. You worry about them and think about them all the time unnecessarily.

Example:

Mindy was a woman with traits of Preoccupied Attachment. She was very dependent on her husband, idealized him, and became preoccupied and angry with him because he was unavailable. She felt that he preferred his work and working out rather than being with her. Mindy got pregnant and had a baby hoping this would help her marriage.

She came to one session with her infant who was asleep when she arrived. Mindy was very distraught in the session, complaining that her husband was still unavailable and feeling helpless to change their situation. When her infant woke and started to whimper, Mindy placed a soother in the baby's mouth without paying much attention to her. The soother quieted her for a brief time. After some time, the baby became more unsettled and started to cry. Mindy was clearly annoyed at the baby, reluctantly tried to focus on her and soothe her. In this distracted state, she gave the baby a bottle and turned back to continue discussing her husband. Her baby remained upset, clearly needing the attention from her mother. Mindy was unable to set aside her needs and give full attention to her baby.

If you continue to ignore your children, they may believe they have to be more demanding and express their needs and wants from you in a more dramatic form. This dynamic may become more toxic as you grow angrier, and they are more demanding. This could lead to your being more punitive and aggressive in your parenting.

In your angry state, you and your child may shut down any loving and pleasurable feelings and remain distant from each other. Your child may eventually get frightened by your cold and rejecting behaviour and try to find ways to pull you back into more closeness. If you remain angry and don't respond, your child may become even more frightened by your distance and try more strategies to engage you. This could include faking illness just in the hope that you will care for them again.

You may need your child or children to take care of you, be a friend, or to meet your needs through their activities. You may do this because of your tendency to be dependent and your hope that your children will help you feel whole. This is not and should not be the role of the child in a healthy parent-child relationship. You may be more at risk of this inappropriate relationship with your children if you are a single parent, have a partner/spouse who is not emotionally available, or your marriage has ended in separation or divorce, and you are left with custody of the children.

Here is an example from one of my cases that I mentioned previously. Sonia was a Preoccupied Attached Adult who was extremely dependent on her husband. When the marriage was deteriorating, she became more dependent on her son to take care of her and to help her understand what happened to her marriage. She was relentless in her demands on her son and constantly shared her preoccupations about her ex-husband with him. Her son became annoyed but tried to put limits on his mother with some empathy and understanding. Eventually he became enraged at his mother, smashing a wall, and banging the table when I saw them in therapy. He explained to me that he had also expressed such anger at his mother when he was a child because of her demands on him and her inability to focus on his needs and feelings in any consistent way.

You may be overindulgent with your children because it is difficult for you to set limits and deal with the anger or disappointment expressed by your children.

An example of this is Jack, who is very inconsistent in the parenting of his children. Limit setting is based on his mood rather than the behaviour of his children. At times he sets limits with empathy and firmness, at times he does not bother to enforce the limits he has set, and at other times he enforces them with anger and punishment. His children do not know what to expect so generally either ignore the limits and rules or fear their father when he starts yelling and punishing them.

You may feel threatened by the relationships your child has with other adults or peers. If you need your children to be your companion and meet your adult needs for emotional closeness, you may feel threatened by these other relationships, such as a relative, teacher, their peers or even your spouse.

Another client of mine who has a Preoccupied Attached Adult was envious of the relationship her children had with their father. She recognized that he was a great father and was able to be patient and loving with their children. But at times she resented their attachment to him and her perception that they preferred him to her. She would be threatened when they would leave her and run to him when he came home or did not run to her when she came home.

Another client described her mother as very involved in all her activities. She went to every sport practice and event, travelling with the team if necessary. Although everyone thought this mother was a great parent, my client experienced this mother as involved for her own narcissistic needs. She longed to go on trips without her mother accompanying her.

Think about all the parents who are on their smart phones while their children try and get their attention. Children with preoccupied parents will call "Mummy" in a normal voice at first and then start to be more insistent in their calls. Mummy, mummy, MUMMY, MUMMY, MMUUMMY. The child may end up screaming at their mummy until finally the mother puts away her phone and pays attention. Next time you are at a mall, listen to the sounds of mummy or daddy repeated with growing loudness, stress, and anger.

Most Preoccupied Attached adults have difficulty trusting others and are highly sensitive to someone not being available to them. The anxiety and anger that results from this feeling of not trusting others usually is directed to other adults but can also be directed at children. You may understand rationally that you need to be consistently available to your children and put their needs and feelings before your own but practicing this will be difficult for you. You may already have demanding, anxious, needy, and angry children. They may present such behaviour because they believe that the best way to get your attention is to be dramatic and emphatic in their demands.

In time, you may withdraw from your child because you are exhausted by their demands, their defiance, and their aggression toward you. You may ignore your child or leave him or her or them to go to your room for a break. You may be so angry at your child that you lock yourself in the bathroom, in the bedroom, or leave the house. When you do this, your child may become frightened by your withdrawal and anger. Your child may realize that somehow, he or she has pushed you too far and now you are not available. Your child may become more loving and charming to pull you back into the relationship. But let's assume you are still too angry to reconnect with your child. Then your child needs to try more drastic measures to force you to pay attention. He or she may claim to be sick or hurt, so you cannot ignore her. You may then come out of your room to take care of your child. Your child may settle, and you and your child feel close and loving. This connection will not last because neither of you have changed your basic belief that no one is consistently available. Your child will continue to try many manoeuvres to ensure you are available and close to him or her but will eventually become angry and mistrustful again.

It is important that you understand that you developed your Preoccupied Anxious Adult Attachment because of your own early childhood experiences. I hope you will be able to work on yourself, resolve your issues from your past, and develop a more Secure Adult Attachment. This would ensure that your personal changes occur at a deeper level, and that you earn your security. With this earned security you will be emotionally available to your children more consistently. This deeper kind of work may mean you have to go into your own therapy. Change at a deeper level takes time but your children still need to experience you as available and empathic to their needs and feelings. So, while working on yourself and being kind to yourself, in the process, I am offering some areas to work on in your parenting.

The first steps are stages in your own self-awareness and ownership of your struggles to help you be less angry at your children.

Understand that it is hard for you to focus on the needs, wants, and feelings of your children when you are feeling that your needs are not being met by your partner, your spouse, a close friend, or your parent(s). Your brain will automatically start to develop thoughts about your intimate adult relationships, and you may become preoccupied with thoughts and feelings about the unavailability of these people.

You must work extremely hard to stop the rumination about such people not meeting your needs. You can do this by forcing yourself to focus on something else such as your work, an activity, reading a book, watching TV, or anything that can distract you from your preoccupied thoughts. In time, you will figure out what works for you and use these strategies to stop the ruminating and unproductive thoughts in a timely manner.

You will need to consider, with honesty, your involvement in your children's academic and extracurricular activities. Are you involved to support and encourage your children or for your dependency needs, and your difficulty developing your own interests and sense of self? It is important that you work on becoming an autonomous person, with security and pride in your own accomplishments, whatever they are.

You will need to work on regulating your emotions.

Your awareness and acceptance of your Preoccupied Attachment, and the emotions and thoughts that do preoccupy you, will help you be different with your children. If you truly accept that your adult attachment is part of your personality and parenting, you may be kinder to yourself and less angry at your children.

I will offer more exercises and guidelines on changing your parenting as an adult with a Preoccupied Attachment in Chapter 5.

Dismissing Attachment and Parenting

If you placed yourself in the Avoidant/Dismissing Category, you will have different challenges in relationships and parenting than people with other adult attachment types.

The following are characteristics and behaviours that you may have or display:

- You probably have great difficulty with intimacy and may not feel emotionally close to anyone.
- You value your independence and your successes.
- You may not be aware of your emotions or, if you are in touch with some feelings, you have difficulty expressing them.
- Feelings of being vulnerable, sad, or anxious will be most difficult for you to express
- You may be more comfortable expressing feelings of anger since such feelings do not leave you feeling vulnerable.
- You may not feel emotionally close to your partner/spouse or to your children
- You are more comfortable being involved in your work, your profession, and/or your extracurricular activities, than in close relationships or in relaxing and just hanging out with people.

- Being successful and excelling in your work and activities is paramount, so you devote most of your time to your profession or work and your activities
- You may have difficulty in sexual relationships or not understand the emotional intimacy that sexual relationships include.
- You tend to figure out problems on your own, rather than discussing them with your partner/spouse, friends, or even colleagues. You develop and act on your own solutions.
- You may come across as secure, confident, and stable. This is based on your successes and achievements and presentation of a calm and contained personality. Underneath this appearance you are a person who is afraid of closeness, who does not trust others to be unconditionally accepting, and who may feel lonely and alone.

Example:

Ken was a successful entrepreneur, who was attractive, fit, and comfortable in social settings. He appeared to be a confident man, clear about his goals, able to take on new challenges and make important decisions with assurance. He was married with a young child. After developing trust in his therapy with me, he revealed that he felt very alone and unhappy in his isolation. He shared that when he was young, he would go to the lake near to where he lived and contemplate terminating his life to end the pain of loneliness.

Some of the strengths you will have as parent with Dismissive/Avoidant Attachment are:

- You are usually rational so may make good parenting decisions, particularly during stressful times with your children.
- You may be a good balance to your partner/spouse who may be more emotional and dysregulated in their parenting role.

- You may be successful financially so can provide financially for your children and ensure they have a stable and comfortable lifestyle.
- You may value and enjoy the involvement of your children in sports and extracurricular activities, so you ensure you participate in these activities.
- You may be supportive of their academic success and engage in their school activities.

However, the strengths you display as a parent may also be your limitations or setbacks. You may have the following challenges and/or behave in ways that are not helpful to developing trust and security in your children:

- You may have a difficult time being attuned to your child. This means it will be challenging for you to understand the feelings and needs your infant and child has and may be expressing in certain behaviours.
- You will tend to focus on the behaviours and try to deal with the behaviour rather than what the behaviour means and the feelings and needs underlying the behaviour.

For example, a family came to me for therapy because the son, Ronny, 15 years of age, refused to attend school. Ronny had done well in school until he received a poor mark in one subject. He was well liked by his peers and successful in extracurricular activities. The father, Jean, demanded that his son get out of bed and go to school. He was furious that his son refused and would just cry. The father would storm out of the house and stopped talking to his son. The mother felt helpless to intervene. They eventually came to me after trying other forms of therapy.

I learned that Jean believed he had to be the best student when he was a child and worked extremely hard to get into the best University in his country. He did not. He was accepted into the second-best University and never forgave himself for this failure. Jean continued to focus more on his career spending more time at work and travelling for his job than at home with his family. He felt that making the time to be involved in his son's academic performance and other activities was him being an involved parent. In the family session, Ronny was able to say that he felt like a failure after receiving a poor mark and was now fearful of failing in school. He felt that he could never be a good enough student for his father.

When I reflected to Jean that he was passing on to his son his own belief that he had to be the best to be accepted by his parents, he began to cry. He was able to acknowledge his own shame at not being the best and his wish, therefore, for his son not to have this feeling. I recommended that Jean have individual therapy as well as continue in family therapy. In their work in therapy, Ronny slowly began to attend school and his mother began taking a more active role in standing up to her husband and supporting her son's own wishes and needs. Jean was reluctant to attend individual therapy but did offer more support to his son in family therapy.

- You may not spend quality time with your child/children. You may go to work early in the morning and not return until late, missing times with your children at breakfast, after school, and at bedtime.
- You may not feel the lack of closeness with your children, but they certainly will and wish they had a more involved parent.

Another client, Jeff, also believed he had to be the best lawyer in his firm and worked diligently to become a partner. He wanted a family and was thrilled when his wife became pregnant with their first child and later a second. His wife remained at home to take care of the children, giving up her own career. In time she became very resentful when she realized her husband was not available to her or the children. He did provide a good income, but his wife felt burdened by the demands of their children. Both children had challenges in school and were hostile to their mother. She demanded that her husband get involved with the children and he did start to take them to their hockey games in the evenings. He could not understand why his wife was so angry at him and why his sons were not thriving in school. He believed that the lifestyle he provided for them should enable his children to be successful. He was angry and puzzled that his wife did not appreciate all that he did for the family. He did not understand that what they all needed was his emotional involvement.

- You tend to focus on the achievements of your child rather than accepting them unconditionally. Unconditional acceptance does not mean you do not have expectations on your child to do well at school and in other activities, but your expectations are based on the interests and abilities of your child, not on your needs or your social status.

Most of us know about the celebrity parents in the United States who paid to have their children accepted into the prestigious schools. These parents needed their children to look like high achievers although their children did not excel academically and did not merit acceptance to such schools. These parents had the funds to create false achievement records and buy their children's acceptance into the schools. The message to their children was twofold: they were not good enough achievers for their parents, and they did not have to be since their parents could buy their entrance into prestigious schools.

- You tend to be authoritarian in your parenting, focusing more on rules, routines, behavioural expectations, and consequences and punishments. I am not in any way suggesting that rules, routines, and expectations are not important. They are an important aspect of parenting, but these should be implemented to make your children feel safe and to encourage your children to be the best they can be. If children are not following routines or not doing well in school or other areas, it is important that a parent explore and understand what his or her child is feeling and experiencing rather that punishing them for their behaviour.

I worked with parents who had adopted siblings. One of the brothers had great difficulty in school. He would lose his homework assignments, lie and state that he did not have any homework, and resisted doing any work during his homework time. His parents were adamant that he sit and do his homework and became angry at him for not concentrating and making some effort to do schoolwork. I worked with these parents to be less concerned about the schoolwork and focus more on their emotional connection to their son. They had an exceedingly difficult time doing this. Both parents had been high achievers in school and in their professions. High achievement was important to them. They could not understand why their son did so poorly at school when they knew he was intellectually capable. They could not be playful and affectionate with him since he was so resistant to their demands on him. They would deprive him of enjoyable activities if he did not do his assignments or homework.

There may be other ways you need your child to meet your adult needs rather than you meeting their needs, engaging in their interests, and being emotionally available for your child. You may need your child to tell you how beautiful you are or how wonderful you are or what a great parent you are. You may be a person who needs to look beautiful and spends a great deal of time on your makeup, your hair, your clothes, or shopping for all these items. Your child may learn that he or she must put aside his or her or their needs and wants and make you feel beautiful or special. If your child gratifies this self-absorbed side of you, you will pay attention and appreciate them, but the attention you offer is based on your needs, not on the needs of your child.

An older woman, we will call Rickie. spent her whole life self-absorbed in how she looked and how charming and entertaining she was. Rickie could not pass a mirror without looking at herself and primming. Her son, Mike, learned to meet these needs of his mother and would tell her how beautiful and wonderful she was. He made her feel needed, valued, and special when he did this. Her daughter, Maddie, learned early in her life that her mother was not attuned to her needs and so she tried to become more independent. Maddie tried to please her mother by being successful, by organizing family events, and being the caregiver of her mother as she aged. However, Maddie could not flatter her mother in the way her mother needed, did not engage with her mother in her superficial needs for beauty and appearance, and generally was not the daughter her mother wanted. Rickie was very rejecting of her daughter and constantly critical of her.

If you are aware that you are a parent with a Dismissing Attachment, you will need to work on becoming more secure by understanding your own childhood history. You will also need to work on your parenting by being more emotionally available to your children and less focused on their performance and achievements. I will explore this more with parenting practices in Chapter 6.

Unresolved/Disorganized Adult Attachment

Parents with an Unresolved Adult Attachment typically suffered major losses as a young child or trauma from parents/caregivers who were extremely neglectful or physically, emotionally, or sexually abusive.

Such people remain unresolved about this early trauma and thus are disorganized emotionally and neurologically and, as a result, disorganized in their parenting. They will respond to their child based on their emotional state, rather than the behaviour or needs of their child. They also may be triggered by the behaviour of their child, the age or developmental stage of their child, the emotional needs or demands of their child, or other issues a child may have. They may be triggered by other people involved in the life of a child.

For instance, if a mother was sexually abused by her father when she was young, she may be triggered when her child becomes the age when she herself was abused. In this triggered state, the mother may distort or misinterpret the actions of or discussions with her child. She may interpret normal behaviour, such as her adolescent daughter becoming more interested in boys, as dangerous. She may accuse the father of sexually abusing their child, particularly in a divorced situation. She may become overprotective of her child's interpersonal relationships. These are overreactions prompted by the mother's unresolved trauma.

This may be an unusual case, but it does reflect the point that even a loving parent may be a danger to her children if she has not resolved her sexual abuse. I did a custody and access assessment of children who were presenting with symptoms of sexual abuse. The parents had separated, and each wanted custody of their sons. The mother was accusing the father's girlfriend of sexually abusing their children. This girlfriend presented as the most stable and empathic adult in the lives of these children. I extended my assessment because it was difficult to determine who, if anyone, was sexually abusing these children. After a period of time, I gained the trust of the children. They told me that it was their mother who was involved in inappropriate sexual behaviour with them. I learned that this mother had been abused by her father and never resolved the effect on her. She loved her children, but her lack of resolution made her a danger to her children. The children were removed from her custody and full custody was given to the father and his girlfriend.

If you are a parent with unresolved trauma, you may be unpredictable in your responses to your children. Your children may develop their own Disorganized Attachment because the responses from you are erratic and at times frightening. Children need to turn to a parent/ caregiver for comfort and safety if something is frightening them. If it is you, the caregiver who is the source of the fear, young children do not know what to do or who to go to for protection. They may run from you, fight back, or just freeze and do nothing. All these responses are not healthy and indicative of a traumatized insecure child.

Barbara, a client of mine, had a mother who had serious mental health issues. At times she was fun and loving and other times she was angry and rejecting. Barbara and her sisters could not predict her mother's moods and reactions. They were always anxious and at times frightened by their mother. Their father had abandoned the family when Barbara was a young child. Barbara grew up always feeling nervous and unsafe and needing to scan her environment for danger. When Barbara had children of her own, she had not resolved her early trauma. She continued this unresolved pattern in her parenting and was unpredictable in her reaction to her own children. Her children had significant mental health problems. Barbara came to therapy as an older adult, finally wanting to resolve her early issues and to be a more stable mother to her adolescent children.

If you are a parent who uses alcohol or drugs to cope with your unresolved trauma your children will become vigilant so they can recognize when you are in a state of intoxication or high on drugs. They will know that they are not safe during these times. They may stay away from you, hide from you, or take care of you during your inebriated state. Your older children may protect your younger ones and become caretakers when they should be receiving care from you.

I once worked with an adolescent female, Katie, who was being adopted by a young couple. Her mother had been an alcoholic and drug addict. Katie had learned to take care of her mother and her younger brother for many years. She would put her mother to bed when she was drunk. She would feed her brother, put him to bed, and ensure they were both up to go to school. When she saw that her mother's anger and unpredictable behaviour was hurting her brother, Katie contacted child welfare and she and her brother were taken into care. Katie felt guilt and deep sadness that she had abandoned her mother. She had little trust in adults to take care of her and believed she had to be self-sufficient and independent. Katie took years to trust her adoptive parents.

If you are a parent who suffered neglect and abuse as a child and never resolved this, your first task as a parent is to go into therapy to resolve your abuse. This is the first step in preventing your abuse from impacting on your parenting and from transmitting your unresolved attachment to your children.

Such therapy may be long term and involve very painful disclosure about your experiences. You will need to ensure you are living in a safe environment and have a relatively organized and predictable life.

If you are married to or living with a partner who is abusive, you will need to leave this relationship before doing the tough therapeutic work. You should not uncover your traumatic experiences unless you are feeling safe and have good supports in this challenging journey.

You will also need to ensure that your children are living in a safe, structured, and predictable environment. You will have to make great effort to provide this environment while you work on becoming a secure parent. You will have to find people whom you know and trust to be available to your children when you are feeling disorganized and not able to parent your children with empathy and emotional control.

If you continue to parent them with unpredictable behaviour, at times being emotionally or physically abusive and at other times being attuned and kind to them, you will pass on your Unresolved/Disorganized Attachment to them.

Parents who have been abused as children and then chose a partner who abuses them may also allow their children to treat them badly.

Joanne came for therapy because she was having difficulty with her adolescent boys who were having trouble with school and were particularly challenging to their mother. She complained that they were very disrespectful to her. In the family session they were critical of their mother, dismissed any of her concerns about them as exaggerated, and challenged her that she spent too much money on herself. The father, Neil, did not intervene to stop them. It became clear that Neil was also critical of Joanne and would be verbally abusive to her in front of the children when he was angry. Although Joanne presented a story of her childhood that was idyllic, I knew that she must have experienced some form of negative parenting to tolerate the emotional and verbal abuse from her husband and children. In the family sessions I helped Joanne assert herself with her sons and her husband. Eventually, Joanne and Neil came for marital therapy. I learned that Joanne felt she was never good enough for her parents and that her father was an alcoholic and at times abusive. Although Joanne had been successful in her profession, she constantly felt like a failure and did not feel entitled to be treated well by others.

If you suffered loss as a young child, you may have a Disorganized or Unresolved Adult Attachment. Most of the adopted children I worked with suffered loss of their biological parents. Most of them had been infants or toddlers when they were placed in orphanages or foster homes. The adoptive parents and I tried to help these children understand that their parents gave them up either because they had mental

health issues, were ill, were unfit to parent, or due to financial limitations. Many of these children believed they were placed in orphanages
and adopted because they were unlovable, even as infants. This belief
that they were unlovable and could be abandoned again resulted in the
mistrust of their adoptive parents and helped to understand their defiant and rejecting or detached behaviour. They had Disorganized
Attachments.

If this loss was not resolved by adulthood, these children would
become parents who continued to believe they were unlovable and
remained hypervigilant to being rejected or abandoned.

*Carl was a client who was extremely authoritarian, often angry, and
punitive with his wife and children. He became paranoid if he did not
know the whereabouts of his wife and was threatened by any friendships that she had. He would either become enraged at her or withdrew into his work for days at a time. His behaviour was very
frightening to his children.*

*His wife, Abbie, told me that Carl had been raised in an orphanage.
He refused to discuss this in his therapy, denying this experience had
anything to do with his present problems. In time, Carl became more
trusting of me and allowed me to explore his early history. His mother
had placed him in an orphanage shortly after his birth. He believed
she was a prostitute and could not care for him. She visited him in the
orphanage, but he knew her only as this lady who on occasion came
to see him, bringing gifts. Eventually she stopped visiting. He did not
know the reason.*

*Carl was able to reflect on the impact on him of this loss and on his
survival in the orphanage. He had been a compliant, well-behaved
child in the orphanage. He was liked by the other nuns and children
and given responsibilities as a leader in the orphanage. One nun had*

expressed maternal love for him. He was discharged from the orphanage into society at 16 years of age and found a room to rent. The owner of the rooming house was kind and supportive of Carl and encouraged him to pursue a career in the newspaper business.

Carl cried as we discussed his sad early history. He recognized that his mother had placed him in the orphanage for his well-being. She attempted to stay involved. By understanding his childhood trauma, Carl was able to appreciate that his relationship pattern with his wife was based on his fear that she would abandon him. She was able to reassure him that she would never do this. Their relationship improved and in time, Carl was able to allow himself to be vulnerable, expressive, and more trusting with his wife. He became more sensitive in his parenting and his children gradually grew to trust his emotional regulation.

Chapter 5

PREOCCUPIED ADULT ATTACHMENT: CHANGING YOUR PARENTING

This chapter includes exercises and guidelines to change your parenting if you are a parent with a Preoccupied Adult Attachment. These guidelines are not a replacement for the work you need to do on yourself, perhaps in therapy, to become a securely attached adult but will help you practice some better ways of parenting your children. It is important for you to realize that you can prevent your children from developing an insecure attachment by being aware of how you parent and by working hard to change those aspects of your parenting that will limit the secure development of your children. For parents with a Preoccupied Adult Attachment the most significant challenge is being consistently available to your children and putting aside your own dependency needs.

The following are exercises for you to try. Take your time to do them and do not become discouraged if you initially cannot succeed in doing them well. These are guidelines for your parenting until your children have grown into adults.

Focus on the needs, wants, and feelings of your infant or child and try not to personalize their behaviour and challenges.

Infants will communicate their needs in instinctive ways. They typically cry, make sounds, wave their arms and legs, and make eye contact to tell their caregiver what they need. The caregiver who pays attention, figures out what the infant needs and responds in a timely manner will be able to calm them. Once the infant is calm and regulated the caregiver can find pleasure in the interface with them. Infants only become more agitated and louder in their cries if the caregiver is not paying attention to them.

You may be able to focus on the needs of your infant and child much of the time and get pleasure in playing with, communicating with, and just being with your child when you feel good and feel fulfilled in your own primary relationship. The challenge will be when you are not feeling good about yourself or when you are worried about the love and attention from your spouse, partner, boyfriend/girlfriend, or parent(s).

When you hear that your infant is crying more loudly and more stressfully, or your older child is calling you in a more demanding voice, stop what you are doing and more importantly stop the preoccupations in your brain. Your child is signaling to you that you are not paying attention to him or her and that they need you to do this. It may feel to you that they are demanding and annoying but tell yourself that they are young and really need you to give them your full attention. When you become fully present to your children, they will calm down and be less demanding. They calm down because you are showing them you are available and attentive. It will take time and effort to practice consistency and availability. It will take time for your child/ren to trust you to do this.

Let's explore further the case of Mindy that I mentioned in the previous chapter. I may have been able to be more effective in helping Mindy focus on the needs of her infant in her session with me. I could have done this if I had been empathic to her feelings of anger at her husband and her desperate need to talk about this. I could have assured her we would have time to talk about this in her session and encouraged her to halt our discussion, temporarily and to focus on the needs of her infant. I may have joined her trying to settle her infant so she would feel my support and presence. I suspect that with my empathy and attentiveness to Mindy, she could have focused on the needs of her infant and settled her infant. This intervention would have allowed Mindy and I the time to focus on Mindy's needs.

If you are in an emotional state where you are irritated, angry, and frustrated, you must calm yourself before responding to your child. If your child is an infant or toddler, you may not have the luxury of taking the time to calm yourself but do the best you can. Tell yourself your infant needs you to respond calmly and empathically and, if you can manage this, your infant will become calm as well. If your child is older and has the capacity to understand that you have different needs, wants, and feelings, you can tell your child you need a moment to finish what you are doing and then will be there for him or her or them. This may be the minute you need to get yourself organized emotionally so you can be calmer when you come to them. Your acknowledgement of your children and their needs confirms for them that you are paying attention. This confirmation will enable them to tolerate your unavailability and absence.

If you have told your child that you will be available in a short time, you must follow through with this. This is an important change in your parenting to regain your child's trust. Be consistent in your availability and follow through on the time you stated you would be available. Your children need to rely on your consistency and predictability to develop security.

Example:

9-year-old child:

"Mommy, mommy, mommy, I need you. I can't decide what to wear to school today. You said you would pick something with me last night and you didn't. I need you NOW. I can't decide whether to wear my white top with the flowers or the blue one. Where are you? I need you NOW. I hate you. You never come when I need you. It will be your fault if I am late for school."

Dialogue between child and mother with Preoccupied Attachment:

"Julie, I told you I am busy with Paul (younger son). He is younger and needs help putting on his clothes. You can wait a minute, for God's sake. I told you to pick your clothes last night, but you were too busy talking on the phone. It's your fault you can't make a decision now. I will be there in a minute."

Julie (screaming now): "Mom, I need you now. I have to go. OK, I am going to wear the dirty sweater I had on yesterday. It's your fault I will look terrible. I hope the welfare comes and takes me away because you don't take care of me."

Mother (exasperated): "I am here. You are acting like a spoilt brat. Here, wear this one. It doesn't matter anyway. You think anyone cares what you wear? Just get ready. We have to leave in 5 minutes. Next time plan what you are going to wear the night before. I am not going to come running in the morning when you don't know what to wear."

Both leave for school angry and upset.

Dialogue with a Securely Attached Parent:

Julie: "Mom, mom, I can't decide what top to wear today, the white or the blue one. I should have checked last night but I forgot. I have to leave in 5 minutes."

Mother: "I tried to get you to do this last night, sweetheart, but you didn't get off the phone. Let's learn from this that it is better to figure out what to wear the night before. I am helping your brother at the moment but I will help you decide. Bring the tops here and we can figure out which one you want to wear. They both look good on you."

Julie: "Thanks, mom. I'll be there in a sec."

If you feel that you are too angry to engage with your children, try and find someone else to take care of your children while you take a break. This can be your partner/spouse, your parent or your mother/father-in-law, or a friend. Let them know that you are having a difficult time and need them to help with the children. Your spouse or partner may have to leave work, but you may have to insist they do this for the needs of your children.

Use this time to take some space from your children, if possible. Go for a walk, write in a journal, meditate, go shopping, talk to a friend, take a nap, or do whatever will help you calm down. You may need and want to talk to your spouse/partner or whomever has come to help you with your children. You must put the needs of your children first. Tell yourself that you will be able to talk to this person after your children are napping or sleeping. Delaying this need will be hard for you so allow yourself some other distractions.

Once you have calmed down and feel more able to deal with your children, do so as soon as possible. The timelier you can reconnect with your children and be available for them, the more likely it is that they will trust you to be consistent with them. Your children need to feel this to develop their own capacity to control their emotions and to develop more independence from you.

Elaine, the woman I mentioned previously, who was so inconsistent in setting limits with her children, did learn that she needed to call her mother or husband when she was so stressed and angry at her children. Since she already called her husband frequently, she and her husband had to work out how she could communicate when she absolutely needed him for the children, rather then her daily dependency on him. If her husband could not leave his work, she would call her mother, with whom she was overly dependent. Her mother would arrive, but always made Elaine feel incompetent. By understanding this dynamic with her mother, Elaine could leave her children with her mother, and use this time to calm herself, do something enjoyable, and make herself feel better. By the time she arrived home, Elaine could cope better with her children and not be so affected by the negativity of her mother.

If no one can give you the break you so desperately need, you will need to develop strategies to calm yourself. You will need to learn breathing exercises, distractions from your intense feelings, and self-talks that are positive.

Perhaps you already have medication that you use to relieve your anxiety. You may need to take this to help your brain boost the calming chemicals it is not producing adequately enough. You may have to talk to your doctor or therapist about getting a prescription for medication that helps reduce your anxiety. You may need to accept that, until you are able to change your Anxious Preoccupied Attachment Category or learn behavioural strategies that work for you, you may need to remain on medication that helps ease this anxiety and preoccupation.

Only a physician can help you make this decision and prescribe appropriate medication.

If you have older children, you can explain to them during a calm time that you have difficulty regulating your emotions and being consistent. You can assure them that your difficulties are not their fault but that, during your emotional times, it would be helpful if they were able to manage their needs and feelings more independently and let you find ways to calm yourself. Assure them that as soon as you can calm yourself, you will interact with them again in a more caring and fun way and be fully present for them. This may be difficult for your older children since they probably already believe that they need to intensify their feelings and demands to get your attention. They may mistrust your capacity for availability and feel the need to cling to you. Talk to them about this mistrust, reassuring them you will do your best to find time to be fully present for them.

Example with Julie and Mother:

Julie: "Mom, mom, MOM, MOMMMMMM."

Mother: "Julie, I know you feel that you need me right now, but sweetie I am feeling very upset and angry. This is not a time I can be helpful to you. You will have to figure out which top to wear. Both look good on you so either will be fine."

Julie angrily picks a top, puts it on and stomps downstairs.

Mother: "Julie, you know sometimes I get upset, yell at you, and make you feel I don't want to be with you. This is not your fault. Sometimes I have so many other worries on my mind that I can't pay attention to you. I am sorry about that. Today I am having a bad day. But I promise you that, while you are at school, I will calm myself and work *on the problems I have. When you come home, we will do something nice together. We may have to include your brother, but I will see if Mary can come over to babysit so you and I can do something, just the two of us."*

Julie nods but clearly does not trust her mother to follow through.

Mother: "I know it is hard for you to trust me to do this. But I will do my very best to make sure I am in a better mood when you come home."

Being fully present for your children when they need you is essential if you are going to help them develop security. For this reason, you must accept that your adult attachment of Preoccupied makes being fully present or available to your children a challenge. Their demands for this, their excessive dependency on you, and anger at you is the result of your inconsistency with them. And your inconsistency is your legacy from your early childhood experiences.

You have an opportunity to break the chain of generational transference of attachment. You can begin the process of enabling your child or children to develop Secure Attachment by owning your insecure adult attachment, by working hard to change this, by working hard to parent differently than you were parented, and by being kind and forgiving of yourself when you slip back to your insecure methods of parenting. Say sorry to yourself and your children and try again.

Sonia, my older client who needed her children to be more attentive to her needs than theirs, eventually began to accept that she did not appreciate everything that her adult son did for her. With her growing independence and self-reliance after her divorce, she was able to appreciate her son's availability and understand that she was disappointed because of her own need for more consistency. With her greater autonomy and expressing her appreciation to her son for his attentiveness, their relationship improved, allowing her more access to her grandchildren. Parental change can occur at any life stage.

If you are overinvolved with your children and cannot tolerate their independence from you, you will need to work on finding other activities, other areas of involvement, and other relationships to offer you meaning in your life. Your overinvolvement with your children usually happens because your sense of self was overly dependent on your relationship with your parents. You did not learn to value your other accomplishments or friendships.

Sonia was also overly enmeshed with her mother. She had done well in school, went to university, and became a teacher. She always felt insecure in her profession. When she married, she immediately gave up her career, became enmeshed with her husband and his needs, and only valued their joint endeavours and activities. She never developed her own friendships, her own interests, and her own sense of self. She continued this pattern in her relationship with her children, expecting them to meet her needs and becoming angry when they asserted their independence and left her out of their activities.

By understanding her adult attachment and recognizing her overdependency on her children, Sonia gradually began to develop her own friendships and activities.

Chapter 6

DISMISSING ATTACHMENT: CHANGING YOUR PARENTING

∽

This chapter offers you some parenting strategies, specific to your Dismissive Adult Attachment. Given your propensity to achieve and be the best at whatever you do, you will have to contain this drive and just do the best you can with these guidelines. When you are unable to complete an exercise to perfection, focus on what you have achieved and allow yourself to fall short in some other areas.

Here are some of the areas you will need to change as a parent.

You will have to let go of all the activities that you have developed to avoid closeness in relationships. This may mean that you will have to leave work, not go to the gym or other activities, and go home to be engaged with your children. If your child is an infant, this will be more challenging since infants have more primitive needs and cannot engage in more adult-like activities. This may be less satisfying for you as a parent. If you are a professional woman and have worked hard to achieve a leadership role, you will have conflict between your professional ambitions and your parenting. Remember, in the early years, no one can substitute for you in the development of your child's security.

You will have to sacrifice some of your professional ambitions to be available to your child.

I recall that, when I was pregnant, I was concerned about how I would balance my professional ambitions and my parenting responsibilities. The Executive Director of my agency was a successful professional woman who also had children. To my surprise she strongly encouraged me to return after my maternity leave on a part time basis. She assured me my position would not be compromised and that, when I was ready, I could return full time. I realize that not all women have this privilege, but I was grateful that I could remain more available to my child. When I did return to work, even part time, it was excruciatingly painful to leave my child. However, I was able to be fully present for her in her first year of life and believed she had a secure attachment to me.

At times I had to force myself to leave work to be with my child. I was still concerned that I was not offering enough time to my profession and my agency. At times I left because I had to pick up my child from the nanny or daycare, but I was still thinking about my cases at work or dynamics with other colleagues. When I look back on this time, I realize I needed to free my mind of my working thoughts and be fully present for my child. This may be what you need to do.

Examples of conversations:

The Dismissing Parent:

This may be the conversation that a Dismissing Attached Parent would have when picking up her young child from daycare.

Parent: "Hello, Mary (Daycare staff). How was Diane today? I hope she was well behaved. (Going to the child who is not running to her mother) Hi sweetie. I hope you had a nice day. Where is your backpack?"

Child: "Mommy, we watched a movie."

Mother (distracted): "That's nice, dear. We have to get home quickly so I can prepare dinner."

Mother just focuses on getting her child organized so they can leave.

Child, leaving with her mother: "But mommy we watched this movie about Mary Poppins. She was like magic. And Evan, pushed me and I cried."

Mother, driving home: "That's nice, dear. I need to call your father to tell him to pick up some things on the way home."

Mother, at home: "Ok sweetie, put away your backpack. Why don't you go and watch TV while I get dinner ready? Your dad is picking up your brother and will be home soon. I hope your dad won't be late, as usual."

Same conversation with Secure Parent:

Mother arrives at Daycare. Child runs to mother.

Child (3-4 years old): "Mommy, Mommy, we watched a movie today and Evan pushed me, and I cried."

Mother, hugging and holding her child: "Wow, it sounds like a lot happened today. I know what. You can tell me all about the movie in the car when we go home. Let's talk with Mary, (the daycare staff) about Evan and you?"

Child: "Yeah, I cried, and Mary talked to Evan.

Mother and child talk to daycare staff so mother is well informed and can comfort her child.

Mother, in the car: "I am sorry that Evan hurt you. I'm glad you told Mary so she could help you and make you feel better. Do you want to talk more about it?"

Child: "No. I want to tell you about the movie. It was Mary Poppins and there was all this magic."

Mother listens. Asks questions and shows interest in her child's excitement about the movie.

Mother, at home: "Let's put away your backpack. Do you have anything to show me from the daycare? (Child does not have anything). I have to make dinner. Why don't you come and sit in the kitchen and tell me more about your day? You can draw some pictures or colour in your book while I make dinner. Daddy and your brother will be home soon."

You may need to learn how to be empathic and attuned to your child, rather than focusing on behaviours and performance. This means coming home and asking your child how they are feeling about their day, about their friends, about their schoolwork and their activities. You need to focus on feelings, not performance. If your child is having difficulties in school, you need to ask about their feelings on not doing well, their understanding of why they are struggling, their feelings and their thoughts about what would be helpful. As a parent with Dismissing Attachment or traits of this, being in touch with your own feelings may be difficult so accessing the feelings of your children will also be challenging. You will have to practice not asking your children about their marks, how many goals they scored, how many parties they were invited to and generally not asking about their activities with an emphasis on success.

This is typically the content of a discussion with a child from a parent with a Dismissing Attachment:

Father: "Hey Bud, sorry I got home late. I had to finish a big project at work. I know we planned to play a game of basketball but this job was too important. So how was school today? Any great marks to tell me about. How did you do in that test you had last week?

Child: "Oh, hi Dad. Yeah, mom told me you had to work late. I just threw the ball myself for a while. Yes, school is fine. I did okay on the test. Hey Dad, I'm busy on my computer now. Can we talk later."

Dad: "Yeah, sure son, but what do you mean you did okay on the test? I thought you said you studied hard for it and would do well."

Child: "Yeah, well, I didn't do great. Can we talk about this later?"

Father: "No, I want to know about it now. It's important you do well in school if you want to achieve in life. And you have to get great marks to get into the best universities one day. So, what was your mark?"

Child: "Dad, I did okay, and I don't want to talk about it now. I know all about getting good grades and I'm not worried. And I still have time to get great marks. I am only in grade 8."

Father: "You obviously don't understand if that is your attitude. Now is the time you learn to study and impress all your teachers. In fact, have you done your homework and what other tests are coming up?"

Secure Parent and Child

This is the conversation a more secure and attuned parent would have and one that you may learn to have. Your child will come to believe they can trust you, share their concerns with you and do well in school out of a feeling of security and belief in himself/herself.

Father: "Hey Son, I am so sorry I got home late and missed our time together to play basketball. I was really looking forward to it and am so disappointed that I had to miss it. I did everything I could not to stay late because you are important to me. I had to finish this project. I hope you were able to throw some balls, even if I wasn't there."

Child: "Thanks, Dad. Yeah, I was really disappointed, but mom told me you had to work late and couldn't get out of it. She told me how sorry you were. I also wanted to talk about that test I did. I didn't do so well. But Dad, I just want to finish this game on the computer."

Father: "No problem, Son. I am going to change and have a bite to eat. Let me know when you want to talk. I am sorry you didn't do so well. You must be disappointed. I am happy to talk about it and see how I can be helpful."

In the first conversation the father is only focused on his son's performance and putting pressure on his son to achieve. He does not recognize his son's disappointment at his father not being available to him nor does he focus on his son's feelings about not doing well on his test. His already knows that his father does not give priority to the relationship with him, believes that he must be the best to win his father's love and does not trust he can share his own disappointment and worries about his performance. His son likely will develop an Avoidant Attachment similar to that of his father.

In the second conversation, the father is empathic to his son's disappointment at his coming home so late and shares his disappointment at not playing a game with his son. He is clear in his communication to his son that he values and gets pleasure from the relationship with his son. He also communicates his awareness that his son is upset by his test performance and will be available to process this when his son wants to. This father places the needs and feelings of his son before his own.

If you have a more challenging child because your child has ADHD, is on the spectrum, adopted or reacting to difficulties in the family or in your marriage, you may feel angry, and frustrated that you cannot manage your child. As a Dismissing Attached adult, you may have read books and articles on your child's area of difficulty, may have taken courses, joined parent groups and tried, without success, many of the techniques and parenting interventions recommended. If these were not successful, you may feel helpless and useless. These are difficult feelings for Dismissing Attached parents and may result in feeling depressed and withdrawing from your child. You may blame your child for causing your feelings of incompetency.

Feeling vulnerable, helpless, and frustrated is normal at times for all parents but more so for parents of challenging or special needs children. You will have to learn to allow these feelings and seek support from your spouse or partner, friends, or other parents. You may need to go into therapy to have a safe place to express these feelings and learn to accept your own limitations.

Some of the behaviours and conditions of your children may not change and you will have to learn to accept the neurological compromises of your child and understand that he or she is doing the best he or she can.

Example:

Years ago, I had a client, Jill, who had adopted a toddler from an international orphanage. Jill had been a highly successful professional in a financial company. She and her husband were unable to have biological children, so they adopted. She was looking forward to this adoption. When her adopted child arrived, at 18 months of age, he was a difficult child who did not easily attach to this mother. All her hopes and dreams of being a wonderful mother, close to her adopted child, were shattered. Jill tried various strategies to engage her child, without success. She fell into a serious depression, rejected her child and eventually was unable to function. She felt deep regret that she had given up her career to adopt a child.

Jill was referred to me and I was able to help her mourn the fantasy she had of being a perfect mother. We were able to work on her need to be perfect in all the activities she pursued, whether professional or personal. She was placed on anti-depression medication from her doctor. In time Jill was able to understand that she had post-adoption depression, felt inadequate as a mother and was angry at her child for instilling this feeling in her. She gradually felt better, was able to function, able to allow herself to be imperfect and focus on the challenges of her adopted son. She eventually understood that he arrived with these challenges and that his difficulty attaching to her had nothing to do with her. He needed time, patience and her empathy from her. She needed to understand that his fear of being close was based on his fear of being rejected by her. In time he was able to trust his mother but continued to have cognitive challenges. Jill no longer personalized his struggles and offered the support he needed.

Eventually, Jill became a leader in the adoption field helping other adoptive parents who were depressed and feeling helpless to parent their adopted child.

It will be easier for you to focus on rules and consequences and ensure these are implemented. It will be more difficult for you to focus on understanding why your child is challenging the rules, breaking the rules, or defying you. You may become angry at your child for disobeying a rule, implement a consequence and never talk with your child about their feelings and experiences. You may just remind your child about the rule and consequence and warn them there will be a worse consequence if it happens again. What is most important to you is that your child obeys you and accepts your rules and expectations. However, what is more important is the reconnecting with your child after the consequence.

When we are angry at our children for breaking a rule or defying us, there is a break in the relationship. None of us feel love for our child in the moment when we are angry at them. Our children feel this rift as well. Repairing the break in the relationship as soon as possible is imperative. Otherwise, our children feel deep shame rather than feeling badly about their behaviour and learning from their experience. Feelings of shame are devastating for one's sense of self. Children who feel shame are not able to examine their behaviour, share their feelings, learn from the experience, and reclaim their closeness with a parent. We want our children to feel badly about breaking rules or getting in trouble and reflecting on their behaviour. They also need to know that you, as a parent, will not reject them, will be willing to talk and resolve the issue that caused the problem. I will discuss this more fully in Chapter 9.

Examples:

Adolescent child has broken the curfew and come home late. Child is 15 and curfew on the weekend is 11 pm.

Conversation with adolescent child and Dismissing Attached Parent:

Parent: "Where the hell have you been? Do you know what time it is? You were supposed to be home at 11 pm and it is now 1 am. Go to your room. I can't even look at you, I am so disgusted. You are a big disappointment. You are grounded for the rest of the week. I don't want any of your lame excuses. Go to your room."

Next morning at breakfast: Parent does not look at their child and does not speak to the child. Clearly parent is still angry.

Child: "Dad/Mom, I am sorry about last night."

Parent: "I don't want to hear your excuses. Don't do it again. Next time you will be grounded for a month."

Conversation with adolescent child and Securely Attached parent.

Parent: "Where have you been? I have been so worried. I am so relieved you are home. Are you okay? Did anything happen to make you so late?"

Adolescent: "Yeah, sorry, mom. I know I was supposed to be home at 11 but all the kids stayed late, and I had to wait for Jack so we could call a taxi together. His curfew is 1 am. Most of the kids have later curfews. It's not fair I have to be home at 11 pm."

Mom: "I know it is hard for you to have an earlier curfew, but we talked about this, and I thought you understood and accepted why we have our curfew. It is too late to talk about this. We can talk more about this in the morning. You are grounded for the week. I know you feel angry about this, but you know that is the consequence. I am sorry you made the choice you did. I hope you get a good night's sleep. You look tired and I know you want to sleep in. You won't be able to do that because you have to be up for your practice in the morning."

Next morning:

Mom: "Hi sweetie, I am happy you are down for breakfast this early. I know you must be tired after getting home so late. Do you want to talk more about this? I am not prepared to change your curfew, but we can talk about how I can help you to tell your friends that you have to be home at 11."

Adolescent: "Mom, I am the only kid who has to come home so early. Well, not the only one. But most of my friends can come home later.

Jack's parents don't care when he gets home. Please mom, can't I come home at 1 am? You are so unfair."

Mom: "I am sorry you feel that way. I know that lots of your friends have the same curfew because I am friends with some of the parents. I really like Jack and I feel badly for him that his parents are so permissive and don't seem to care where he goes or when he comes home. I will never be that kind of parent with you. We discussed your curfew, particularly on Friday night, when you have to be up early for your practice on Saturday morning. If you need a ride home, you can always call me. I will come and pick you up wherever you are. You are grounded, sweetie, since that is the consequence for your choice to come home after your curfew. We can talk more about his on the way to your practice, but you have to get ready now."

You will need to explore the needs and wants of your child/children and give priority to these. As a Dismissing Attached parent this may be a challenge for you. You may be more focused on your social needs, your interests and your personal wishes and ambitions for your child. You may have found ways to justify why you neglect your child in favour of what you want to do professionally or personally or forcing your child to do what is your need and interest, rather then theirs. Your children may have learned to deny their own needs, wants and feelings, believing they will get some attention from you if they please you and meet your needs and wants.

Examples:

Young child and Dismissing Attached parent.

"Mommy, can we go to a movie today? Nadia's mom took her to see The SpongeBob Movie. *She said it was so good. I want to see it."*

Mother: "I have to go shopping today so you are coming with me. If you behave, I will buy you something nice."

Child: "Ah mom, I don't feel like going shopping. We went last time and I didn't have fun. I don't want to go. It's not fair that I have to go."

Mother: "Well, I have to get some things at the mall. Sharon, your nanny, is off today so you have to come with me. Otherwise, I would leave you at home. Take your iPhone so you can play some games while I shop. I don't want you to give me a hard time like last time. I need a new dress for my friend's party. You want me to look nice, don't you?"

Child: "Yeah. You always look nice, mom. Okay. I'll play my games. Can we go see the movie another time?"

Mother: "We'll see."

Young child and Securely Attached mother.

Mother: "Sweetheart, I know you hate going shopping with me but I have to get a dress for the office party. Maybe, we can find some fun things to do at the mall while we are there. Is there anything you would like to do?"

Child: "Oh, mom, I don't feel like going shopping. I want to go to a movie. Nadia said that SpongeBob Movie is playing and she said it was fun."

Mother: "I know you don't like shopping, sweetheart, and I wish I could go another time. But I have to buy the dress today, so you are stuck with me. And you can tell me which dress you like and which you don't. I would like your opinion. We can see if the movie is playing at the mall and if we have time we can see it. I don't think we will have enough time. But there is your favourite ice cream place in the mall so you can get an ice cream cone."

Child: "Okay. Can I get a chocolate marshmallow ice cream cone?"

Second example:

Adolescent child plays hockey. Father with a Dismissing Attachment leaves work to bring his son to the hockey game and watches him play. His son is not playing the game well and misses some scoring opportunities. His father is yelling at him and his coach during the game. This is an example of a dialogue after the game.

Son, looking defeated and scared of his father. "Sorry, Dad, I missed a couple of shots. I promise I will do better next time."

Father: "What the hell happened to you? That was the worst playing ever. I can't believe I pay for your hockey lessons and your fees for this league. You don't deserve to play. You better improve your game, son, if you expect me to keep paying. If I had the opportunities you do when I was a child, I would have become a professional hockey player." (Father goes on to tell his son how he needs to improve his game.)

Dialogue between adolescent son and Securely Attached father.

Son: "Sorry, Dad, I know I played a lousy game. I can't believe I missed those shots. I think the coach is really angry at me."

Father: "I saw you were having a difficult time. I know you must be very disappointed in your performance. I have seen you play better so wondered what happened. You don't have to apologize to me. But let's talk about what happened and how you can improve so you feel good about your performance. I am happy to be with you when you talk to the coach if you want me there."

You may have difficulty being a comfort and support to your child when they are upset, sick or hurt. You may believe that it is important to toughen up your child, so you don't "baby" them when they are feeling upset or vulnerable because of something that happened to them. You may be able to provide practical advice or do practical acts if your child is sick or physically hurt. You can make soup, let them stay home, wash a wound and put on a band aid. You may not instinctively take your child in your arms or on your lap and cuddle them for comfort. You may not let your child just cry and express how upset they are or tell you about the incident that upset them, without intervening and giving advice. One of the important indicators of a secure child is one who can turn to a parent for comfort and support, no matter what their age.

There is an example of the reaction of a Dismissive Parent in an autobiography written by Hilary Clinton. In the story, Ms. Clinton presents her parent's reaction as positive in preparing her for life's challenges. She describes the history of her mother, so we are sympathetic to how her mother survived a deprived childhood and learned to take care of herself.

Hilary Clinton describes an incident when she was four years old. A girl across the street was rough with Hilary, who came home crying. Her mother had witnessed the incident and stated: "Get back out there and if Suzy hits you, you have my permission to hit her back. You have to stand up for yourself. There's no room in this house for cowards."[6]

Hilary understood that her mother was afraid that, if Hilary gave in to her fears, it would set a pattern for the rest of her life. Her mother's intent was to make Hilary strong and able to stand up to children that bullied her. I believe the pattern it set was the transfer of her mother's Dismissive Attachment to Hilary Clinton.

---

6 Clinton, Hilary Rodham, *Living History*, 2003, Simon & Schuster, New York, pg. 12.

Here is how I wish her mother had responded.

Hilary, four years old, running into the house crying and telling her mother that the girl across the street was mean and rough with her. Her mother had watched the episode.

Mother takes Hilary into her arms and listens as Hilary describes what Suzy did to her. "Oh Sweetie, I am so sorry that Suzy was mean to you. I know she can be rough when she plays."

After Hilary stops crying and is safe in her mother's arms:

Mother: "We need to make sure that Suzy doesn't hurt you again. I want you to feel that you don't have to be afraid of her. What do you think we should do? I can go and talk to her mother. Or you can go outside and tell Suzy that she can't hurt you anymore. I can watch from outside our house or at the window. If Suzy is rough with you again, I will come out and stop her. I won't let anyone hurt you, Hilary."

Parents need to protect four-year-old children from harm. Children become secure and able to stand up to bullies as older children when they know they can turn to their parents for protection and comfort. Children need to know it is normal and acceptable to feel vulnerable and frightened at times. These feelings do not imply the person is weak and easily bullied. Secure children will go to teachers and other adults for comfort and protection when they are frightened and expect the adult to offer them guidance and safety.

I believe that, if Hilary Clinton had a more empathic and comforting mother, she would be a strong but warmer and more emotionally available person and politician.

Chapter 7

UNRESOLVED ADULT ATTACHMENT: CHANGING YOUR PARENTING

♋

I f you placed yourself in the Unresolved/Disorganized Category, parenting will be very challenging for you. People in this category experienced significant loss, abuse and/or neglect and have not resolved these experiences. You will need to work on yourself in therapy, so you understand the impact your abusive childhood had on your development and work hard to undo the damage and pain this causes you.

However, you can change some of the harmful responses to your children by understanding and working hard to practice different ways of parenting. Your awareness of your adult attachment and efforts to change will create an opportunity for your children to develop secure attachment.

The following are guidelines for an Unresolved/Disorganized Adult Attachment.

Try and figure out which behaviours or emotions of your children are disorganizing or triggering for you. Your reactions are the result of unresolved issues from your own childhood. You may find yourself suddenly becoming angry at your children, or sad and depressed, or fearful and vulnerable or all the above in a short time. Write down which behaviours or emotions exhibited by your children activate what behaviours or emotions in you. Keep a journal so you can be aware of the behaviours that are triggering for you. For example, you could write: 'when my child screams at me and says he hates me, it makes me feel rejected and unloved." You may be surprised and confused by your reactions. Understand that your unpredictable or intense reactions are not in your conscious awareness. They come from memories stored in the unaware part of your brain.

As you read your journal entries, try and see if there are patterns in your children's behaviour and expressions and your reactions.

When you are clear about these patterns, work on modulating your reactions. You will need to learn calming exercises, mindfulness, and grounding techniques. You may need to leave the situation and calm yourself before rejoining your children and responding to them. Your nervous system is dysregulated from your trauma so learning to settle your nervous system is vital to your parenting and your own mental and physical health.

When you respond impulsively and/or inappropriately, you will need to explain to your children at their level of understanding that you are upset about other matters not related to them. You can apologize to them about taking it out on them. If their behaviour deserved a reprimand or consequence, you must do this in a calmer state with a consequence appropriately based on their behaviour, not on your mood.

Example:

I had a client, Maureen, who had been sexually, emotionally and verbally abused by her father for many years. Any loud voices caused her to become emotionally disorganized. She described feeling frightened, angry and overwhelmed, both wanting to flee the situation and fight. Feeling so overwhelmed she froze and did nothing.

When her children, who were 10 and 12, were squabbling over a television program, their loud voices activated her trauma. Although they were having a normal children's dispute, Maureen overreacted, initially screaming at them to stop fighting, crying, and then running to her room, overwhelmed by her emotions and experiencing a panic attack. Her children, upset by their mother's reaction, immediately stopped their dispute, became very frightened and silent. They felt responsible for upsetting her. They remained quiet, then went to their mother's room, apologizing for upsetting her and begging her to come out. In time their mother emerged from her room, but nothing was discussed or processed about the episode. The children remained shut down and fearful, watching their mother anxiously.

Given that Maureen is unresolved about her early trauma and still must parent her children, the following may be a more helpful way for her to respond to her children.

Children squabbling over which TV program to watch. Maureen is aware that she is becoming disorganized inside. She can feel a barrage of emotions that are developing very quickly. Before responding to her children, she takes some deep breaths, trying to regulate her emotions.

Maureen: "Hey guys, I can hear that you are getting angry at each other, and it is upsetting me as well. Let's see if we can work this out by talking about your different choice of shows. Let's just all take a deep breath and calm down before talking." Neither child can do this well and each starts to tell Maureen that the other sibling is not cooperating.

Maureen starts to get angry and tells her children: "Ok kids, I see that you are having a hard time calming down so we can talk. I am getting angry as well and I need to calm down myself if I am going to help you. You can either sit quietly with me or go to your rooms. Which do you want to do?"

Both children agree to sit with Maureen and stay quiet. Both children sit close to Maureen, and they all start to control their breathing. Maureen works extremely hard to set the example by her deep breathing and becoming calmer. She knows that, if she can be calm, her children will feel this and use her composure to settle their own emotions. In time with Maureen's help, they are able to reach a compromise on the TV shows to watch.

Maureen leaves her children watching TV and continues to work on grounding herself.

If you, as an Unresolved/ Disorganized Attached parent, do become activated by your children, and do not handle the situation with them well, it is important that you discuss your reaction later, once you are more regulated and composed. Your reaction may have frightened your children and have caused a major rift in your relationship with them. It is vital that you repair this. I will talk later in the book about this concept of rupture and repair. This means that your children feel alienated from you, feel terrible about themselves, may feel responsible for the rift and too ashamed to know how to mend the rupture. It is your job as a parent to mend this falling-out and ensure your children feel loved and good about themselves again. You can always revisit the situation that caused the rupture and talk about everyone's reactions, without blame and shame. You can tell your children that you know that sometimes you can be frightening for them, and you are sorry about this. You can share that you are working on being calmer, but this will take some time.

I mentioned a client of mine, Sandra, who had been sexually abused by a boarder in her home when she was young. She would become triggered by her husband when he said something complementary to her about her appearance. Because of her childhood abuse, she believed her body was flawed and damaged. She could not tolerate any reflection about her appearance, particularly when she was feeling vulnerable. When she was triggered, she would explode, screaming at her husband, throwing things at him and eventually running from the house, at times with the intention to drive somewhere. If her husband took the car keys, she would become more enraged and leave the house totally out of control.

In this state of rage, she was oblivious to her children witnessing the conflict and her frightening behaviour. She was usually a sensitive and stable mother. Her children would be frozen in fear during these episodes. At times her older son tried to protect his younger brother from his mother's rage. After my client ran from the house, her husband would talk to the children trying to assure them that their mother would be fine and return soon. He spent time with the children, but he was so upset and concerned about the safety of his wife that he was not able to be very comforting to them.

When Sandra returned, she would be cold to her husband but tried to engage her children in some playful activity. Her youngest was so relieved to have his mother present that he played with her, never asking about the events that happened. Her older son, who was concerned about the impact on his father, remained distant and unengaged with his mother. In time he did re-engage with his mother, longing for the warmth and affection she could offer. He remained guarded about getting close to her for fear of the explosive episodes.

In therapy, Sandra was able to explain to her husband that his compliments were triggering and not helpful, even when she stated how she hated her body. She helped him recognize that all she needed was his empathy and recognition of her feelings, regardless of how distorted they were.

Sandra, with great shame, had to acknowledge the harmful effects on her children that her rageful episodes caused.

The is an example of a conversation she had with her children.

"Joey and Sammy, (not their real names), I want to talk about what happened earlier this evening. I know how scary I was when I got so angry at Dad and ran out of the house. I am so sorry about this. I know it may not help but I want to try and explain what happens to me, so you know that it is not Dad's fault or yours. It is important that you know, in no way is it your fault. Some bad things happened to me when I was a little girl and sometimes, I feel so upset and angry inside because of these bad things. Sometimes Dad says nice things to me, but I don't believe them and don't want to hear them. I get angry, not at your dad but at the bad person that hurt me. I get all confused inside and have to run away. I know Dad and you guys worry about me when I am gone. I promise I won't hurt myself and will come back as soon as I am calmer. Your dad and I are talking about my feelings, and we are going for help so I won't get so angry and frighten everyone.

"I want you to know that you can talk to me about your feelings and worries when I get so mad, but I have to make sure that I am calm and can listen to you. Okay? I love you and will try not to upset you so much. Do you want to ask my anything now?"

Parents with Unresolved/Disorganized Attachment have the greatest challenge to change their Attachment to one of Earned Secure because the memories of their early childhood may be buried deep in their unconscious. These memories and feelings may have been activated in their present life for the first time because as a parent they see how vulnerable their young children are. This realization may bring pain, sadness and anger as unresolved parents consider their own childhood and the abuse or loss they suffered. Retrieving these are very painful yet this is necessary to become a more secure parent. If you are in this category, you will have to do this slowly, ensuring you are not overwhelmed by the feelings and memories.

You may wonder why your parents did not protect you if you were abused by a family member or someone outside the family. You may wonder why one parent did not protect you if you were abused by the other. You may wonder why the authorities and other people in your life did not protect you if they were involved.

All these questions and thoughts are very valid, but your first goal should be to ensure that such abuse or neglect does not happen to your children. You may promise yourself that you will never be like your abusive or neglectful parent but, if you do not resolve your own trauma, you will have difficulty providing a safe and secure environment for your children. Your unconscious beliefs that relationships are not safe, that you must be vigilant so no one hurts you, that you are not worthy of love and nurturing will interfere with your wishes and intentions to be a good and loving parent.

Your Unresolved Attachment may be so severe that you sometimes dissociate so you are not aware of your surroundings or don't recall what you have done or where you have been. If you know that you dissociate at times, you must ensure that other people are available to your children. When you know that you are severely triggered and feeling chaotic and frightened, you must contact someone you trust to be with your children. These reactions to being abused or neglected are less common but are most harmful to children who may not know where a parent went or when they will return and in what state they will return. They do not understand the behaviour of a parent. Such reactions are terrifying for a child when they are helpless to do anything to help a parent and cannot protect themselves from that behaviour.

Sandra, the parent I mentioned in a previous example, did resolve in her therapy much of the damage caused by the sexual abuse she suffered and was able to become a more stable and sensitive parent.

Chapter 8

THE VALUE OF BEING
A SECURE OR EARNED
SECURE PARENT

This book encourages you as a parent to become a Secure or Earned Secure adult through therapy and/or hard work on yourself. You can earn or gain a sense of security in yourself and in your relationships by:

- Examining your own childhood history with brutal honesty
- Understanding how your upbringing affected your personality, both strengths and setbacks
- Accepting with compassion your limitations and compromises and maybe those of your parents
- Working hard to change both in your therapy and in your daily life

Parenting is more pleasurable and less problematic for Securely Attached adults. This does not mean that Securely Attached parents do not have challenges. Parenting does bring challenges, with both children who have special needs and children who do not. Even secure parents experience anger at their children, disappointment, sadness, fear and anxiety. Secure parents typically experience emotions with better regulation than insecure parents. They can reflect on the feelings evoked by their children, understand the source of the feelings and react in a more rational manner. Secure parents have integrated brains with emotions, thoughts and actions working in a collaborative process.

Dr. Main termed the word Autonomous for adults with Secure Attachments. I am not sure why she chose this term as it seems to emphasize independence and separateness. Yet, securely attached children and adults develop the capacity for both independence and intimacy. We know how important it is that children feel they can leave their parents to explore the world, to have new experiences, to develop new relationships and to grow from such experiences. Children also need to feel they can return to a parent when the experiences in the world are frightening, confusing, stressful, painful or when they simply feel ill or have physically hurt themselves. Adults also need to feel this.

Secure adults feel a sense of autonomy that allows them to feel safe and to trust in their strengths, capabilities and independent decisions. Such adults believe they can rebound from stressful or even traumatic events and to accept their personal limitations without self-judgment. They trust that they can turn to an intimate other when they require emotional support, practical advice or just a caring person when they are ill or physically hurt.

Some of the other qualities that Autonomous Adults and Parents have are:

- They value relationships and make time for close relationships
- They understand that adult relationships are mutual where they may have to delay getting their needs met for a period of time without feeling angry and resentful
- They are able to develop mutually satisfying close relationships
- They turn to others when they need emotional or physical support
- They are able to accept the autonomy of their spouses, partners and children and are not threatened by other relationships

- They are able to resolve conflicts in relationships without feeling threatened that conflict will destroy a relationship
- They are able to express needs, wants and feelings in a balanced manner
- They are able to be sympathetic, empathic and understanding of the needs, wants and feelings of other adults and their children

Most adults who have secure attachments have been raised in a stable loving environment. As children, they would have experienced the consistent love and support of at least one parent. They would have been able to go to this parent when they were feeling sad, frightened, upset or physically hurt or not feeling well. The parent would have offered comfort for both emotional and physical needs. This means that a parent would not only offer practical help for a sick child or child that fell and hurt themself but would offer emotional support by holding a child and comforting them with hugs, kisses and soothing words.

Unless a tragic event or events happened to such an adult, this adult would be able to parent his or her child in a secure environment as well, offering all the elements that would contribute to the child developing a secure attachment. There are times when traumatic events do happen to secure adults such as wars, forced migration, sexual assault or a pandemic that can disrupt the security of the adult. However secure adults have the capacity to bounce back even from horrific events once the trauma has been resolved or their situation stabilized.

Dr. Main discovered in her research that some parents who had a terrible upbringing presented as securely attached. When she and her colleagues tried to understand this, they realized that such parents had alternative people in their childhood who were loving and secure. Such people were available consistently, were loving and nurturing, and with enough time and intensity, that they made a positive impact on the child. Such alternative caregivers could compensate for the lack of availability or rejection by a parent. These positive relationships would

be internalized and create a positive sense of self and trust in relationships. Examples of such people are a step-parent, a grandparent, a
relative, a teacher, a neighbour or the parent of a child's friend.

I had a client whose mother was selfish and abusive and yet this client
had enough security as an adult. She was a balanced mother, took
responsibility for her part in issues, and worked hard in her relationships with both her child and her partner. When I explored her history,
she told me that she would go to her paternal grandmother on a regu-
lar basis and felt loved and secure in that relationship.

Other people became secure because they worked on themselves either
on their own or in therapy. They were able to acknowledge the negative
experiences they had as children. However, they were able to create a
different meaning for themselves about their upbringing. They were
realistic about the negative aspect of their parents/caregivers and the
impact on their personal development. They possessed a balanced
understanding of the setbacks in their development and the construc-
tive and positive attributes they possessed. By working on their deficits
in a mindful and compassionate way, they were able to resolve the
negative early childhood experiences and emerge with what is called
"Earned Security". This resolution allowed them to engage in life and
relationships in more rewarding patterns. The journey to Earned Security is a challenging one with bumps and stumbles along the way but
well worth the effort.

Let's look at what a parent with a Secure/Autonomous Attachment or
Earned Secure Attachment can offer their children. I have given examples in the previous chapters how a Secure parent will respond to challenges. I will offer some general parenting advantages that come from
being a Secure/Autonomous parent and relate this to the different ages
and stages of development.

Infants and Toddlers

- Secure parents are attuned to their infant from birth and on- ward, in time, coming to know what their baby is telling them with her/his cries and other instinctive signals.
- Secure parents will respond to their baby in a calm balanced manner even when the baby is stressed and cries loudly.
- Secure parents will work at figuring out why their baby is upset, staying calm and soothing the baby.
- Secure parents will know when they are overwhelmed and will ask for help in managing the baby.
- Secure parents will get much pleasure in being a parent and interacting with their baby when the baby is in a happy and playful mood.
- As the baby becomes more mobile a secure parent will be able to encourage the baby's exploration and supervise more closely to ensure the baby is safe.
- A secure parent will be able to allow other people to develop a relationship with the baby, always knowing that they are the primary caregiver and the main source of comfort.
- Secure parents will understand that their toddler will need more independence to explore the world and be curious about other children and people.
- Secure parents will encourage this independence and ensure their availability when the child needs to return for comfort and safety.

A good example of autonomous behaviour can be found in play- grounds. Toddlers will move away from a parent to explore the envi- ronment and the other children. Some toddlers will do this carefully, looking back at their parent/caregivers for reassurance. Other toddlers will do this more confidently but still check to see that the parent is watching. Other toddlers will go forth more impulsively and energetically, forgetting to check on the caregiver.

It is the parent/caregiver's responses that are significant for creating the security of the child. The shy reticent child may need more encouragement from a parent to explore the playground and more assurance that the parent is watching. More confident children will go forth without this push but still need to know their parent is observing them. Children who are more impulsive will need more supervision and guidance and therefore more attention from the parent.

All children will need to go to their parent if they are hurt physically or are upset by the actions of another child. Secure children will have no difficulty going to their parent, but there may be differences in their needs for attention. Some secure children will just look at the parent, know she/he is watching and ready to come and help. These children may be able to get up on their own and return to their playing, just from knowing their parent is available.

Other children may cry when they hurt themselves, need the parent to come to them and comfort them but are able to recover quickly and return to their play. Yet, other children may need more support from the parent, may want the parent to pick them up and hold them for a while. Secure children who need more comfort from the parent can settle within a short time and want to return to their independent play.

Secure parents will provide a structured environment with the balance between routines and flexibility and empathy and limits. They do not need to become authoritarian, trusting their own capacity to set limits, meet the needs of their children and be flexible. Feeling internally self-regulated and confident allows a parent to have fun, go a little wild and break the routine at times.

Secure toddlers are already developing the balance between independence and intimacy with others. They trust their parents are emotionally and physically available and are beginning to apply this trust to other adults in the world.

School Age Children

By the time children enter school they have internalized a secure or insecure attachment from their parents. Even Securely Attached children will have challenges with developing peer relationships, dealing with both good and not so good teachers and learning new subjects and information. Having a Secure/Autonomous Adult Attachment as a parent becomes more significant for parenting school age children since now you, as a parent, have less control over the events and relationships that will influence your child.

Most children with Secure Attachments will be popular with peers and develop healthy friendships. They will gravitate to other secure children and be less interested in friendships with troubled children. They will be liked by their teachers and school staff and be asked to be helpers in the classroom. They will generally perform well academically. If they have learning challenges, they will acknowledge this without being self-critical and accept the help they need. They will engage in extracurricular activities of their own interest and perform to the best of their ability.

Even secure children will have challenges that Secure/Autonomous parents have to navigate.

Generally Secure/Autonomous parents will not personalize the challenges or struggles their child is experiencing. They understand that life will offer encounters that their children will need to face and from which they will need to learn and grow. They trust in their capacity to help their child negotiate the tasks of being a child. They generally trust other adults to be good to their child/ren. They also believe in their own sense of power and ability to advocate for and to protect their child if necessary.

These are examples of the challenges children have once they become school age and how secure parents may handle them.

Secure school age children may have some fears on entering school, particularly if they did not go to daycare or are constitutionally a shyer child. Secure parents will be sensitive and patient, and ensure they are available to their child for support. They may have spoken to the teacher so the teacher can be inviting and supportive of the child. They will also have their own trust in others so will more easily encourage the child to enter the classroom and engage with the teacher. This trust in others will be passed on to their child who will then be able to seek support from the teacher if necessary.

Peer interaction brings challenges to all children, even secure ones. Secure parents will use such challenges to help their child develop more skills in managing the dynamics of peer relationships. Secure parents will explore calmly and, in more detail, what happened in the interaction with another child. They will be empathic to the hurt feelings of their child but also help the child examine their responses and behaviour that may have contributed to the problem. The secure parent will encourage their child to deal directly with the other peer or peers but will know when their child needs their intervention either with another parent or teacher.

If a secure parent does need to intervene, the parent will do this calmly and assertively. Secure parents rarely need to become aggressive. They generate a strong sense of self-worth and command respect from others rather than having to demand this forcefully. Other adults, such as parents, teachers, and principals, will realize this instinctively and more easily negotiate settlements.

This security in the parent in time allows the child to develop his/her own self-worth, always knowing their parent will protect him or her when an adult is needed.

Academic challenges can become an issue for school age children. This is the stage where learning disabilities, attention deficit issues, cognitive delays, autism spectrum symptoms and other learning challenges are revealed. None of these are easy for parents to acknowledge, accept and find proper resources for their child. Securely attached parents will feel all the pain that insecure parents will experience. They will be more capable of bouncing back from this sad and distressing reality about their child and focus on the needs of and resources required for their child.

Both secure and insecure parents may need to advocate for their child, but secure parents do this with a calm forcefulness that does not alienate personnel from the systems that offer resources. As mentioned above secure parents communicate a sense of healthy entitlement that is more likely to advance their causes for their children and to ensure they obtain the appropriate help. Secure parents will create the resources if these are not available and engage other parents in this mission, all done with self-regulation, patience and assertion.

Secure parents will protect their children from other children and adults who may tease or harm their child in other ways. They will do this with the same integration of understanding, patience, confidence, and decisiveness as with all matters. They may use such incidents as opportunities for others to learn about the special needs of their child.

Most important is that secure parents will not personalize their child's challenges or special needs, blame themselves or remain angry or depressed because they have a more challenging child. They will be able to focus on the strengths and specialness of their child and ensure their child also values these.

Secure parents will accept that having a special needs child can be exhausting and painful and know when to seek support from others.

Examples:

My daughter seemed to be a secure child in grade one and I believed had healthy friends at school. I knew most of her friends and to some extent the parents of these children. I was active in her school so knew her teacher and principal. One day, her teacher asked me to stay after school to discus a concern she had about my daughter's relationship with another child. I knew that my daughter was friends with a child we will call Abbie. I knew that Abbie had some problems because her mother was quite honest with me about the effects of her divorce on her and her children.

The teacher described an incident where Abbie had hurt my daughter with a stapler. My daughter had not asserted herself and seemed to accept the aggression from Abbie. The teacher suggested that I encourage my daughter to socialize with other children. I was quite shocked by this event and the reaction of my daughter. As a social worker I understood that Abbie was threatened by my daughter's friendships with other children and had become angry at her. I was reluctant to terminate her relationship with Abbie. I liked Abbie and her mother. However, the needs and protection of my daughter were paramount.

I spoke to my daughter about the episode. She told me she was afraid of Abbie but only when Abbie became angry. She was afraid to stand up to her and had not gone to the teacher for help. My daughter was planning to tell me about the incident but seemed helpless to stop

Abbie. We discussed the importance of going to her teacher for help. I also assured her that I would speak to Abbie's mother and maybe Abbie.

I asked my daughter whom she liked in her class and would like to play with. She immediately said a girl named Stacey. I arranged a play date with Stacey and she and my daughter became close friends for years. Abbie remained a friend of my daughter, but she knew that the teacher, her mother and I would not allow Abbie to hurt my daughter.

I did not personalize this issue although I did become more aware of some insecurities in my daughter. I processed this episode with her, encouraged her to go to the adults in her life when someone else was hurting her and helped her expand her peer relationships. I did not get defensive with the teacher, was sympathetic to Abbie's mother and calmly discussed this concern with my daughter. I could do this because I had developed an Earned Secure Adult Attachment.

Adolescence

Adolescence is a most challenging period in parenting and having a Secure/Autonomous Adult Attachment as a parent is the best protection in surviving this tumultuous stage of development. Adolescents are in such a disorganized state because hormones and other chemicals are developing and causing rapid changes in their brains. The thinking part of their brains is developing but does so in an unpredictable manner. Some days your adolescent will seem calm and rational. You can reason with them and they seem to listen without getting defensive and attacking. Other times your adolescent presents like an emotional hurricane, unable to have a reasonable conversation, refusing to cooperate and stomping out of the room or presenting that silent wall you can't penetrate. You won't know from day to day which version of your adolescent child you will encounter.

What adolescents need during this tumultuous time is a steady, stable and emotionally regulated parent who does not react to the mood of the child. Secure/Autonomous Attached parents are more able to offer this. This does not mean that secure parents don't get frustrated with their adolescent child. But they are more able to depersonalize their child's reactions, understand that their child is struggling with raging emotions and not react to the varying moods and defiant behaviour.

Secure parents also recognize that during adolescence they become less important to their children and are no longer the person or only person the adolescent will turn to for support or advice. Peers become attachment figures and confidants to each other. This is especially true for adolescent girls. Insecure parents may be more threatened by alternative relationships or by the lack of control they have over their teenage children. Secure parents understand this is normal in adolescence and trust that their teenage children will come to them if they are seriously troubled and needing adult comfort or advice. They will also continue to reach out and communicate to their adolescent children although these efforts may be rebuffed. They can do this because they do not personalize the rejection.

Teenagers will emerge from this challenging phase with their own secure attachment strengthened if parents are not reactive, are able to set and enforce limits with understanding and firmness and continue to be interested in and loving to their adolescent children. Secure parents offer this despite their children's lack of interest in them, rejection of them and their adolescent's insistence on independence.

All stages of child development present challenges and worries for parents, both secure and insecurely attached parents. Children with special challenges are even more worrisome and exhausting. What enables Secure/Autonomous parents to handle such concerns, fears and uncertainties is both a belief in their competency and an ease in reaching out to others for help, comfort, knowledge, and advice. They trust themselves and others.

Chapter 9

RUPTURE AND REPAIR

$\mathcal{O}$

The concept of rupture and repair has been written about by several therapists/writers in the field of parenting and attachment. I wrote about it in my previous book, *It's Attachment*, in relationship to how these dynamic impacts conflict in adult relationships. In this chapter, I will expand on this concept because conflict is a normal occurrence in all parent/child relationships. How parents handle and resolve conflict is crucial for the child feeling safe with conflict and believing in resolution rather than feeling frightened and shamed by such experiences.

We all get angry at our children from time to time. When this occurs, the anger creates a rift in the relationship with your child. When you are annoyed or angry and reprimanding your child, you will have difficulty experiencing a feeling of love for your child. You may feel a deep unconditional love but in the moment of frustration this feeling is not accessible. This is normal as the emotional part of your brain is active with feelings of annoyance and anger and the need to reprimand or punish your child for their wrong doings. Your child feels these negative emotions and the distance caused by your anger. Your child may feel badly and respond in a variety of ways: become defensive, get angry at you, cry, leave the situation or run away or apologize and appeal for your forgiveness.

However, no matter how you react initially, it is important that you repair this rift in the relationship and return to the loving feeling you have for your child. Your adult attachment as a parent is going to influence or determine if this repair happens, how this will happen and how fast this will happen. This means that, when there is conflict with your child or children, your adult attachment will determine if your child comes to believe:

- That conflict can be resolved.
- That they can do something "wrong," and this can be forgiven.
- That they are bad children.

These beliefs about themselves and about conflict will be remain at a lasting and unconscious state of mind.

Let's take an example from my therapy practice of a rift that occurred with a child and describe how a secure parent and then an insecurely attached parent would react.

Martha and Harold are parents with two children, Owen and Matthew, aged eight and ten. Martha has a part time job that she does from home. Harold has a stressful job but is a very involved parent. Owen has been diagnosed with ADD and has difficulties concentrating. He often must bring unfinished work from school and protests doing this. Matthew is a better student and more willing to do homework. Harold often deals with the children and with the homework when he comes home from work.

Martha had a difficult morning with the children getting ready for school. She was looking forward to Harold managing the evening routines with the children. Harold called before the children arrived from school telling Martha he had to work late.

After giving the children snacks and letting them relax, Martha asked about homework. She knew that Owen had work he had not completed in school. Matthew said he did not have homework, but Martha encouraged him to look over his math. Doing well in school was important to both Martha and Harold. Owen immediately protested and refused to do his homework. He complained that it is not fair that he gets homework, and that Matthew doesn't. He started to cry and threw down his homework in protest.

Autonomous/Secure Parents

Let's assume that Martha is a securely attached parent. She understands that it is hard for Owen to concentrate and that he often feels he is inferior academically to his brother. She also knows that completing his schoolwork is important for Owen to progress academically.

Owen, yelling and crying at the same time: "I hate this homework and I hate you for making me do it. It is unfair I have to do homework and Matt doesn't. He never gets homework and I always do. I am not going to do it." Owen throws the papers on the floor.

Martha is very frustrated and angry that his teacher did not help him complete his work at school.

Martha: "Owen, you have to do your homework. You did not finish your work in school and your teacher said it has to be done by tomorrow. Now, (in an angry voice) pick up your papers and go sit at the table. I will help you. If you don't do your homework, you will not be able to play with Mark tomorrow."

Owen: "No No No. I don't care what my teacher said. It is not fair, and I am not doing it."

Martha realizes she is becoming very frustrated and needs to calm down. She tells Owen she is going to make herself a tea and will come and help him. During the time she makes herself tea, she takes a few deep breaths, reminds herself how hard this is for Owen and returns to deal with him.

Martha sits beside Owen and puts her arms around him.

"Owen, I know how hard this is for you and I wish it was easier for you to concentrate at school. But sometimes it means you won't finish your schoolwork and must bring it home. Your Dad and I understand this and will always be here to help you. I know it feels unfair to you that Matthew sometimes does not get homework but when he does, he has to do it the same as you. You know we have the same expectations on him. Let's pick up your papers and see what work you have. I will sit beside you but want you to try and do the work by yourself. If you need my help I will be right here."

Owen: "It's just not fair, Mom. I really tried to do the work at school, but Brian started to talk to me and then I couldn't get back to the work."

Martha: "Yeah, it must be hard when there are distractions around you. I know that Brian also has problems concentrating on school-work and sometimes you get caught up with him. I hope tomorrow will be a better day but let's focus on your schoolwork now."

Owen, Sighing and wiping his tears: "Okay. But, Mom, you have to stay beside me."

Martha: "I am right here."

Owen does his work with little help from Martha. They both feel connected to each other, and Owen feels good that he completed his schoolwork.

What this example demonstrates is the ability that a secure parent has in the process of rupture and repair. The secure parent can reprimand their child, remain emotionally controlled, be empathic, be firm about expectations and set a consequence. Martha knew she was already stressed by the day she had and had little patience to deal with Owen in a helpful way. She needed time to process her frustrated feelings after her child refused to do the homework. She removed herself from the situation. Once she was calm, she could be empathic to Owen's difficulties, still insist that he do the homework and be available to help him.

Preoccupied Parents

If you figured out that you are a Preoccupied Attached parent, you know that remaining calm and rational is a challenge for you. This means that, when you get angry at your child for breaking a rule, defying you or just being difficult, you may feel and express this anger with great intensity. The expression of your anger may be frightening to your child and leave them feeling cut off from any closeness to you. Regaining control of your feelings is not easy for you but the longer you take to regulate your anger, the longer your child feels this disconnect and the shame that results from your punitive response.

Let's take the same situation and present Martha as a parent with a Preoccupied Adult Attachment. This is how she may respond.

Owen refuses to do his homework. Martha is still angry from the morning when Owen had difficulty getting ready for school. Martha is also feeling resentful that her husband is working late and that she must be responsible for the children after school.

Martha, angry and losing control: "Owen, I don't want to hear any of your excuses. You know that you have to get your work done in school and when you don't it is your fault. That is why you must do it now. Now pick up your papers before I get really mad."

Owen, angry and crying loudly: "I don't care if I fail in school. I hate school and I hate you."

Owen stomps on his papers.

Martha grabs Owen by the arm and drags him to his room. Yelling at him.

"I have had it with you. I don't care if you do your homework. I will tell your teacher you refused to do it. I hope she keeps you after school and makes you do it. You won't be able to go on your playdate with Mark tomorrow or do anything fun all next week."

Martha slams the bedroom door and leaves Owen crying.

Martha calls her husband and starts yelling at him that he needs to come home.

In this example Martha's anger and lack of empathy for Owen leaves Owen feeling alienated from his mother, badly about his performance in school and perhaps feeling that he is stupid. He defends against these feelings by stating that he does not care about school or his mother. This is not a true feeling. Because Martha leaves Owen in his bedroom without resolving their conflict, he also feels a deep sense of shame that he is a bad child.

The example I gave in Chapter 5 with the mother getting angry at her child for not being dressed and ready for school also can result in this child feeling either a permanent state of being bad or a temporary state of regret. Whether Owen and the child in Chapter 5 will remain in this state of shame will depend on whether either mother can gain self-control, think about the episode, and process it with her child in a loving and thoughtful manner. If the mother can do this, both children will be able to examine their own behaviour and learn from their mistakes. The child who did not prepare clothes the night before may remember to do this. Owen may be able to work harder focusing on school or be more willing to do the work at home. Both children will feel their mother's love and know that their behaviour did not harm their relationship with her

If these mothers cannot examine their reactions, resolve their own anger and reconnect with their child, each child is left with feelings of shame. The child will not be able to look at their behaviour, learn from it and do something more helpful next time. Shamed children remain angry and defensive and do whatever it takes to avoid the feeling of shame and badness.

These are guidelines for the changes you, as a parent with a preoccupied attachment, will have to make, to repair the rupture or disconnect from your child:

- As soon as you feel the initial anger at your child from their disobedience or the challenge to your authority, take a deep breath and step away from the conflict. You have a short fuse so need to know that you have seconds to gain control before your emotions escalate. If you do lose control, yell at your child, and punish them excessively, you will have much repair to do when you calm down. This means apologizing to your child for your excessive anger and spending much time comforting your frightened and chastised child. For your child to learn from their misbehaviour you will need to talk to your child about the reason and importance for your rules and your child's need to take responsibility for his/her behaviour. Your child will be able to listen only if you can remain calm, loving, and thoughtful.

- It is important that you do not personalize your child's misbehaviour. As a Preoccupied Attached parent this will be difficult for you. When you can reason with yourself that your child is not doing this to hurt or abandon you, you will be able to be curious about your child's behaviour and help them look at themselves. Do not shame your child.

Dismissing Attached Parents

Let's assume that Martha and Harold are parents with Dismissing Attachment who overvalue education and doing well in school. This may be how Martha would react to Owen refusing to do his schoolwork.

Martha, with a stern and cold voice: "Owen, I do not want to hear anymore of your complaints and your crying is ridiculous so just stop it. You will sit here until your work gets done. No supper or TV or game time unless your work is complete. Do you understand? It is your responsibility to complete your work at school or do it at home. No excuses."

Martha refuses to listen to Owen and leaves him alone in the dining room sitting at the table.

When his father comes home later, he admonishes Owen as well and sits with him forcing him to do the work. Owen cries but gets the work done. He goes to bed, with leftovers from his dinner, feeling cut off from his parents.

Because Dismissing Attached parents overvalue obedience, performance and achievement, such parents can easily get angry at their children and instill a deep sense of shame in them. If you placed yourself in this category you will have to work hard not to alienate your child when they do challenge your authority, do not perform to perfection or worse perform badly in school or extracurricular activities. If you react with anger, criticism, and belittlement, you will be responsible for the shame that is instilled in your child. I am not suggesting that you should not have expectations on your child to do well in their endeavours. I understand that all parents at times feel disappointed in their children's behaviour and performance and may express this. Children are not harmed by their parents' disappointment or their own disappointment if this is discussed and explored sensitively. Children are harmed by the sense of failure and rejection imbued by an angry and judgmental parent.

The example I offered in Chapter 6 of the father who focused on his son's marks rather than his feelings for not doing well on a test is an example of a Dismissing and harmful father. This father and Martha and Harold all caused a rift in the relationship with their sons by being critical and rejecting and even worse, not resolving this quickly. The boy in chapter 6 knew his father would continue to berate him about his performance and already knew to avoid his father. This boy already had a sense of shame and failure and knew not to turn to his father for support and comfort.

If you know you are a parent with a Dismissing Attachment you will have to work hard to contain your anger and demand for perfection. You will need to demonstrate to your child that you are available to be empathic to their pain and disappointment. You will need to encourage him/her to share their feelings with you and discuss with them how you can be helpful.

These are guidelines to ensure you offer repair after a falling out with your child:

- Own your adult attachment and its strengths and setbacks. Know that allowing yourself to feel vulnerable, self-doubting and imperfect is exceedingly difficult for you so will be equally difficult for you to allow such feelings in your child. If you do find yourself reacting with anger and criticism at your child's behaviour leave the situation. Tell your child you will discuss the event or behaviour when you are calmed down. Do whatever you have found helpful to calm yourself and release your anger. Ensure this is not a strategy that will be hurtful to yourself or your family. Talk to yourself. You are quite capable of being rational, probably too rational, but this is good time to use this part of your brain. You must tell yourself your child is not on this earth to meet your expectations and demands.

- Do not personalize your child's challenges or poor performance. Or their successes. If you want your child to perform well, you need to be available as a supportive and empathic parent. You will need to explore your child's feelings and their understanding of why they are struggling in their endeavours. Be a better listener rather than a problem solver. You need to be aware that responding authoritatively and using only discipline on your child is a guaranteed means of alienating and shaming your child.

Unresolved/Disorganized Attached Parent

Let's assume Martha is a parent with an Unresolved Disorganized Adult Attachment. She would have a difficult time containing her anger and not becoming abusive to her child.

Martha, screaming at Owen: "Owen, I have had it with you. I can't even look at you. You are a complete failure. Just do your homework and stop whining."

Owen looks frightened but does not do his homework. He tries to tell his mother the work is too hard.

Martha slaps Owen. Grabs him and drags him to his room. Matthew watches also looking frightened. Matthew tries to calm his mother.

Martha, yelling at Matthew: "You stay out of this. I don't want to punish you as well, but I will."

In frustration, Martha throws the homework in the garbage. She yells at Owen that he is grounded for the month and will get more punishment when his father gets home.

Martha goes into her bedroom, throws herself on the bed and starts to cry uncontrollably. Owen and Mathew stay quiet, feeling frightened and helpless. They go to bed on their own.

If you placed yourself in this category, you are vulnerable to responding with unpredictable anger at your child's behaviour, a reaction that shames your child. You may not even be aware of why you are reacting in this intense way. Parents with this type of attachment have unresolved issues from their own traumatic upbringing and may be triggered by the behaviour or attitude of their children. Children of such parents are very watchful of their parents' responses knowing that their parents can be unpredictable and frightening. Such children may have experienced many incidents of disruptions without any resolution or repair and already feel much shame and believe they are flawed humans.

You, as an Unresolved Attached parent, have your own deep sense of shame. This will make it difficult for you to examine your responses to your children and own your unresolved issues. It may be easier for you to avoid any discussion about with your child about the conflict and your reaction. But this avoidance will leave your child in a place of fear and shame. So, as painful and shaming as it may feel, you must open a discussion with your children about your reaction, your regret about your response and your reassurance they have not been terrible children.

In chapter 6, I offered an example of an Unresolved parent, Sandra, who had been sexually abused as a child. She worked hard to understand the harm that had been done to her as a child and resolve its effects on her.

With this awareness she learned to contain her rage and to resolve conflicts with her children and husband. She was able to reassure her children that her intense reaction was not based on their behaviour or their presence. She could apologize to them and help them understand her own problems. Owning her problems and reactions helped her children not personalize their mother's extreme emotional and unpredictable responses and be less afraid of her.

I want to reiterate how important it is that you explore your traumatic history with a therapist and resolve the damage that was done to you. I will offer guidelines on how to repair the ruptures with your children, but your own shame will inhibit somewhat your ability to do this:

- Know your triggers. Write down all the behaviours and emotions expressed by your children that activate your intense negative feeling and reactions.
- Once you have an idea about these be aware when you first start to experience them.
- You have very little time to use your rational brain to understand these triggers and gain control of them. This is your goal, but you will need time to achieve this.
- When you know you are losing control and will, in your anger or rage, hurt or shame your child leave the situation, even to go to another room.
- Learn techniques to ground and calm yourself, such as deep breathing, relaxation techniques, mediation or focusing on pleasant experiences,
- Most important of all is that you repair the ruptures that occur with your children while you work on controlling your alienating reactions.
- You must help your children, particularly your older children, understand that you are the one with the problems, not them. Apologize to them and assure them that their behaviour may

have been inappropriate or defiant but not disgraceful. Their behaviour did not warrant your responses of rejection, alienation and condemnation.

- Spend a great deal of time comforting and cuddling your children.
- Work hard on being predictable and consistent in your parenting.

Remember, reprimanding your children and applying consequences for their behaviour in a calm controlled manner teaches them a lifelong lesson that there are consequences for one's behaviour. However, the consequences do not have to be the destruction of a close relationship or the shaming of a child. By demonstrating your love and caring, after you reprimanded your child for certain behaviours, you will teach your child another lifelong lesson. One can have conflict in close relationships, feel anger at another and resolve this. Resolution can allow for a stronger feeling of closeness and the ability to explore the reason for the conflict with each partner owning their part. This can occur without feelings of shame and defensiveness.

This lesson will allow your children to experience conflict and express anger in their adult relationships, knowing that such conflicts can be resolved and do not have to threaten or destroy the relationship.

Chapter 10

MATCHING AFFECT

ℭᎵ

The concept of Matching Affect is one that is commented on in other attachment parenting books.[7] I want to discuss it as well, since it is such an important aspect of parenting. Matching Affect will offer different challenges to a parent based on his or her adult attachment.

What is Matching Affect? When we see a cute smiling baby in a stroller or being held by a parent, we may approach the baby and talk in a babyish tone saying hello and what a cute baby she or he is. When we hear a baby in distress, either our own or another parent's baby, we also use an infantile tone to say: "Oh you are having such a hard time. There, there. Mommy is here or I am here." It is our tone of voice that tells the infant we understand what they are feeling and it is that tone which may be a comfort to an infant. We instinctively communicate our feelings using baby sounds and words. This is an example of Matching Affect.

When I hear a parent reprimanding a stressed infant or child and trying to silence the child, I want to intervene and say: "No, just comfort your child with a soothing voice." Yet many mothers, even of very young infants, become frustrated and irritated by a crying infant and

---

7 Hughes, Daniel, *Attachment Focused Parenting*, 2009, W.W. Norton & Co. New York.

want to silence them. They may start rocking them more strenuously, shove a soother in the infant's mouth or tell the infant to stop crying. None of these moves are effective at soothing the baby. The baby may stop crying only because they come to believe the parent will not soothe and comfort him or her.

I recently witnessed a mother telling her baby to "shut up" and forcing her infant into a stroller where she strapped him in, while he was screaming and fighting her. He stopped only slightly when she held him briefly before forcing him into the stroller. She had no awareness that he needed to be held and would have calmed down if she had continued to hold him and soothe him with her tone of voice. Her stress drove her to shut him down and get him out of the situation where he was disturbing other patrons. I would have offered my help but not sure the mother would have welcomed this.

My daughter recently gave birth. Because I spent much time with my granddaughter in her early months, the concept of Matching Affect became more meaningful and present. When my granddaughter was a few weeks old and wet and pooed in her diaper, I changed her diaper commenting on how good she was going to feel with a clean one. She would coo and make sweet noises. I would coo with her. If she peed while I was changing her, I would laugh, and we both seemed to enjoy the moment. When she was in pain from a gaseous stomach, I used a more concerned and soothing tone to comfort her while I rocked her. It was my tone and affect, not my words, that conveyed to her I understood what she was experiencing, whether this was joy, discomfort or pain. My tone matched her emotional and sensory experiences.

At all ages we welcome the feeling of being understood by another human. We feel comfort when we experience the voice of another person connecting to the feelings we are experiencing. Think about a time when you were sad because you lost someone you cared about.

If someone tells you in a soft and sad-like tone that they are sorry for your loss, you believe they truly get the emotions and mood you are experiencing. If someone uses the same words that they are sorry, but this is expressed in a flat formal tone, you do not feel they are in touch with your internal state.

If you are angry and someone is trying to suppress your feelings or telling you to "calm down," this is not helpful. If someone walks away because they are afraid of or disturbed by your anger, this only increases your anger. If someone does not react and withdraws when you are angry, this is hurtful and rejecting. None of these responses communicate to you that the person you are angry at or the person to whom you are describing your angry experience is empathic to your emotions.

We, as adults, want to be understood, even if our sadness or anger is disturbing to the other person. If someone responds to our anger with awareness and empathy, this response is what helps us calm down and reduces the intensity of our anger. Whatever we are feeling, sadness, anger, fear, loneliness, or vulnerability, we will welcome an empathic response from others and find that our pain or anger is alleviated by such reactions. We feel our feelings are matched.

This concept of Matching Affect has other descriptions or terminology. It has been called mirroring, attunement, mimicking, empathy and emotional understanding. I use the term Matching Affect because it conveys the need to communicate one's awareness of another's feelings by expressing with a similar tone, level of intensity, liveliness or dullness the feelings of the other. This does not mean one has to be feeling exactly what the other is feeling. If a child is angry, the parent does not have to be angry as well to match affect. The parent has to express their recognition of the feelings of the child with the same degree or intensity of expression.

We now understand from research that infants become regulated when a caregiver conveys to the child that they recognize the child's signals and respond accurately. This is usually communicated with sounds and voice tones that help the infant feel he or she is understood. The caregiver also meets the infant's needs, but both the provision of need and the emotional response are necessary for the infant to feel a parent truly understands their internal world. The infant's need for the caregiver to communicate nonverbally, match affect and provide for practical needs continues throughout childhood. Yet this nonverbal response seems to get lost once a child learns verbal communication. Then we hear "use your words" as if nonverbal communication has lost meaning. Receiving nonverbal communication and experiencing the matching of affect from others is a life-long human need.

Parents with Secure Autonomous Adult Attachments will have an easier time matching the affect of their child. Secure adults have a greater capacity to be empathic and less likely to personalize the reactions of their child. In the examples I offered in other chapters, parents with secure attachment were able to communicate to their child that they understood how difficult a task was for their child or understood how frustrated a child was or understood how angry or sad a child was. The parent who conveys this with the same degree of emotionality of the child will be more effective in both helping the child feel understood and in helping their child become more regulated. With such regulation the parent can better help a child problem solve or just achieve a calm state.

The father, in Chapter 6, who conveyed to his son with a tone that conveyed his own sadness and loss at coming home late, was able to help his son express his disappointment. This father was also able to say with a caring and curious tone that he understood his son was concerned about his test results. This boy could communicate his vulnerable feelings and turn to his father for support because this father clearly communicated empathy and non-judgmental acceptance of all his son's feelings. The father who was critical and demanding of his son to perform better, missed an opportunity to connect at a deeper level with his son. Also, this father did not help his son perform better.

Preoccupied Attached Parents

Parents with a Preoccupied Attachment will have a difficult time being attuned to their child and matching the child's affect. Because their own needs take priority, Preoccupied parents miss many moments to connect with the feelings and needs of their child. Because such parents have difficulty regulating their own emotions, they will have difficulty duplicating the emotions of their child.

Yet, if you are a parent with a Preoccupied Attachment, you can learn to do this. It does mean putting aside your needs, feelings and wants and truly tuning into what your child is experiencing. Because you are comfortable with feelings, you have the capacity to do this. Here are some guidelines to be more attuned to your child and match his/her affect so they believe you are in sync with their feelings:

- You will have to control your emotions and practice means to do this. We discussed these in previous chapters. These may include deep breathing, focusing on the present, distracting yourself from your preoccupations and maybe leaving the situation for a brief period.
- Listen attentively to what your child is expressing and pay attention to their nonverbal responses such as their facial expressions and their body language.
- If you find yourself personalizing their reactions or responses, stop yourself from reacting, take a deep breath or take a short physical break and return to reengage with your child.
- As hard as this is, you will have to ask yourself what is my child feeling in the moment.

- If you are having difficulty connecting to your child's feelings and needs, become curious and ask your child if they can tell you more about what they are experiencing. Do this with a calm curious voice. An example of this may be: "I wonder if you can share with me what you were feeling when that happened." Or: "Wow, that must have been hard. Tell me more about what happened."

- Once you feel you do understand what your child is feeling and needing, reflect this back to them with the same quality of expression. Raise your voice, with your control if your child is angry, lower your voice if your child is sad or find your own experience of fear so you can convey this feeling. For example, you may say, in a louder voice than you usually use: "Wow, you sound so angry. I can understand that when I took away your smart phone, you were soooo angry at me!"

If you are able to be in sync with your child's feelings, you will discover your child becomes calmer, becomes closer and more trusting of you and will be able to share with you what they need and want with regulation of their feelings.

You will feel a deeper connection to your child.

But to attain this connection you will have to own and control your own intense affect and learn to control your preoccupation with others for not doing the same for you.

Dismissing Attached Parent

If you believe you are a Dismissing Attached parent, you know that being in touch with feelings and needs and expressing them is very difficult for you. Hearing and seeing your child express feelings may arouse in you, feelings of rejection or even disgust since for you these may be expressions of weakness. Your natural tendency may be to shut down your child's experience of feelings, particularly feelings of sadness, fear, and vulnerability. More likely your child has figured out that there is not much use in expressing feelings and needs since you as their parent are not going to be available to respond to them empathically. Your child already anticipates that you will demean or reject their feelings.

Your natural response to your child if they are upset and struggling may be to offer practical advice or push them to continue a task or activity. If they do not follow your advice or withdraw from an activity, you may also withdraw from them. Your lack of empathy will result in an emotionless connection to your child. Your child will not turn to you for support or comfort, which leaves your child in a sad and lonely inner state.

You can change this if you do understand how challenging it is for you to be aware of feelings and needs and to express them. You need to be both kind to yourself, to work hard on exploring your internal state, to allow for feelings of vulnerability, pain, sadness and fear. I assure you that you will feel a closer connection to your child/ren if you practice the following:

- Stop focusing on the performance or achievements of your child.
- Make yourself more available, even initially to be home and just hang out with your child.
- Start to pay attention to the nonverbal expressions of your child, such as facial expressions or body positions.
- If you notice your child is struggling, looks angry, sad, fearful, or distressed reflect this to them with some expression of a similar feeling. "Hey Mark, you look really sad. Is something bothering you? Do you want to talk about it? I am here to listen. Maybe I can help."

- If your child does not respond because they do not trust you to be emotionally supportive. Repeat your reflection and offer to listen. You could add, "I am sorry it is hard for you to tell me what you are feeling. It makes me feel sad that you don't trust me to share your feelings of sadness. I hope we can both work of our relationship, so you feel safer to tell me."
- Share your own experiences of struggle, failure or self-doubt or whatever experience may relate to the one your child is experiencing. You do not need to tell your child about the resolution, just your feelings of pain and struggle that match their experiences.
- Ensure you have fun and relaxed times with your child, without any focus on accomplishments or winning.
- Understand that changing your relationship with your child will take time. If your child believes you only care about how competently they are doing in school or activities or believes you are not the one to turn to if they are emotionally upset it will take time for your child to change this belief. Stay consistent in being emotionally available and curious.
- Let yourself feel sad and inadequate to create this emotional connection. Continue to try to tune into your child's feelings and let him/her know you want to do this.

Unresolved/Disorganized Adult Attachment

If you have placed yourself in the category of Unresolved/Disorganized, being attuned to your child on any consistent basis will be your greatest challenge. There will be times when you are able to be attuned, match your child's affect, calm your child, and even allow your child to feel safe being vulnerable with you. The challenge for you is that some of your child's feelings and needs will activate your own unresolved feelings and needs. When this happens, it will limit your capacity to be empathic to your child and stay with their need for comfort and support from you. We discussed in previous chapters exercises that you will need to do to be more resolved and not triggered by your children. You may want to reread these chapters.

Having the awareness that your child's expression of feelings can trigger some painful feelings for you is a good beginning to stay with the feelings of your child. Initially you won't be able to tolerate some of their feelings of anger, sadness, fear or any expression of vulnerability. Or you may over identify with such feelings which is also not helpful for your child. If you can accept this, you may be able to sit with your child when they are experiencing such emotions and remain close to them. You may not be able to match their affect or offer them consolation or reassurance because of your own emotional dysregulation. Just be physically close and contain your own feelings. If you can hug your child or touch them with comforting gestures, do this.

It will be helpful for you to know what strategy you developed as a child to protect yourself from your abuse or loss.

Practice the following:

- All the exercises that I mentioned in previous chapters to regulate yourself.
- You do have the capacity to be empathic so believe this about yourself. Your painful childhood experiences have made you sensitive but very vulnerable. Expressing emotions may be dangerous for you.
- Remember that your child or children are just as vulnerable and do not want to hurt you. They long for you to connect with their feelings and make it safe for them to turn to you for support and safety.
- You must work very hard not to let your moods dictate your responses to your child.

- Initially you may miss opportunities to match the feelings of your child because of your own moods and feelings. Be kind to yourself about these missed opportunities. You will have many more.
- If you do recognize that you have been misattuned to your child, you can, at a later moment, acknowledge this with your child, with a sad and regretful tone.

The best action you can take as a person with an unresolved attachment is to engage in therapy to resolve your trauma and/or loss. While working on yourself, work on all the exercises recommended in the book. You may be inconsistent in your parenting, even at times extremely dysregulated. Seek help from others, remove yourself from your children, if necessary and if absolutely necessary, place your children with another caregiver while you work on yourself.

Chapter 11

CONSTITUTIONALITY AND ATTACHMENT (NATURE VS NURTURE)

A ny parent who has more then one child knows that constitutionality or personality differences exist. One child may have been
a difficult and temperamental baby and the other easygoing and calm.
Your first child may have been easy and delightful, so you had another
child, based on this positive experience. Your second child may have
been challenging and exhausting from birth and you may have ques-
tioned why you had a second. Or you may have been fortunate to have
easy going babies. Or, unfortunate, to have dysregulated and difficult
to soothe infants. Attachment theory tells us that, although genes and
constitutionality play a part in the personality development of our
children, the more important influence is the relationship the child
develops with their primary caregiver. So, nurture and nature combine
forces to impact the pathway of your child's development.

Let's consider how a parent's response to his or her baby/child can
influence or modify constitutional attributes. As I mentioned some
infants are born wired to be tense and dysregulated. They may cry
frequently and be difficult to soothe. If this child is born to a dysregulated, anxious insecure mother/caregiver, this child may not have the
opportunity to experience a calm controlled nurturing environment

that would help them become more regulated. The child's developing brain would continue to be stressed and its capacity for regulation continue to be limited.

If this same child was born to a calm secure regulated parent/caregiver who worked hard to provide a soothing and relaxed environment, the child's evolving brain would have a far better opportunity to develop the chemicals and structure for self-regulation and self-soothing. This parent would understand that genetically self-regulation was not a natural trait for her/his child. Therefore, the parent would ensure that their child had a structured nurturing environment throughout childhood. This child, as an adolescent and adult, would learn that they needed structure to feel safe and to perform better and would provide this for themself.

Some babies are born having sensory difficulty with touch and closeness. They pull away from the parent who tries to be affectionate and loving. This would be painful for any parent, but an insecure parent would feel rejected, hurt and possibly angry. They would personalize their infant's inability to accept physical nurturing. The rejected parent would reject their infant in return and this infant would not acquire the sensory development for touch and feel.

Although a secure parent may also feel puzzled and hurt by their infant's rejection of physical intimacy, this parent will be more concerned about their child and explore ways to introduce physical touch and nurturing to their tense infant. This may involve learning in what areas of the body the infant can more easily tolerate touch. This may involve only gentle short-term touching. Most important is that a secure parent will not personalize their infant's struggle and in time help their constitutionally sensitive infant/child to enjoy at least some touch and sensory contact.

In my work with adopted children, I have experienced many examples of how children who appeared constitutionally compromised were able to change their ways of being in relationships. Parents would come to me exhausted and discouraged from an adopted child who would be dysregulated, controlling, defiant, mistrustful and distant. Whether these children were born dysregulated was not known. By the time they were adopted, even as very young children, their personalities seemed formed. Most adoptive parents believed that offering a safe and nurturing home environment would change mistrustful children into loving and trusting children, capable of intimacy. When this did not occur in the time frame the adoptive parents expected, these parents became discouraged, depressed and even angry at their children.

These parents were accurate in their understanding that adoptive children do need a nurturing, safe and unconditional loving environment to change their beliefs. Many adopted children believe that caregivers are unavailable or even dangerous. However, to change belief systems that influence personality takes much time, even years. Those parents who were able to accept this reality and continued to provide the calm and loving environment for years, despite the children's difficulties in behaviour and personality, in time, saw the benefits and changes in their children. These children grew to be more trusting, more dependent and behaviourally more regulated. Eventually, they changed at a deep internal level developing different personalities.

Let me offer you an example.

Sacha was adopted from Russia as a three-year-old by a family who could provide well for him. These parents, Jennifer and John, had two biological children. Their decision to adopt was a clear choice to provide a loving and stable home to an orphaned child. Jennifer felt the need to help a child whose life would be limited by being raised in an orphanage.

Within days of his adoption, the family realized that they had taken on a challenge they had not anticipated. Sacha was very challenging, running around, breaking items, defying any limits placed on him, eating all food in sight and not sleeping. Jennifer felt guilty that she had imposed this difficult child on her family. John withdrew and was not a support to Jennifer. Jennifer began to read about adopted children, the challenges they presented to adoptive parents and the strategies recommended to create a safe home for them. Jennifer had been an administrator in a large firm, was well organized and determined to succeed in whatever endeavour she undertook. She became determined to help Sacha and prove to her family he could be a well functioning member.

Jennifer's search for information led her to the theory of attachment and how adopted children were insecurely attached, some severely so, because of their experiences of poor parenting and their neglect in orphanages. She found an Attachment Focused Therapist and began to understand that she needed to implement structure and behavioural interventions but more important she needed to provide empathy, nurturing, curiosity and consistent love. She also helped her husband and children understand how insecure Sacha was so they could be more patient with Sacha and kinder to him. Jennifer understood that the behavioural strategies were easier for her to implement and had to work at allowing herself to experience her vulnerabilities and feelings of inadequacy.

In time Sacha did calm down, was less aggressive and more open to exploring his feelings. He became very attached to Jennifer. Gradually he allowed John into his circle of intimacy and became a more integrated member of the family. It took years to accomplish this, but Sacha became successful at school, developed good peer relationships, and became a likeable caring and accomplished young man.

All of these changes came about because of the safe and caring environment that was provided for him. We do not know the genetic constitutionality of Sacha since there was little information on his family. He arrived at his adoptive family a very troubled child. We assume, if he had remained in the orphanage, he would have been a dysregulated angry insecure child with a bleak future.

What allowed Sacha to change significantly in his behaviour, in his relationships and his belief in himself to succeed, was the nurturing safe environment that Jennifer and John provided. So, nurture influenced Sacha's neurological development at all levels of his brain. He experienced relationships that were safe so did not need to be aggressive to protect himself. He felt loved and nurtured by his mother and was able to internalize the belief that he was lovable. The safety, consistency and caring provided allowed his cognitive brain to develop so he could think rationally, learn, plan and do well academically. His brain changed and his personality changed. All of these changes were the result of a nurturing predictable environment. Sacha is a good example of how nurture can change personality development.

I offer this example because Jennifer was able to provide the emotional support that Sacha needed to develop trust after she examined herself and allowed herself to feel vulnerable, sad, inadequate, and dependent on others for help. Jennifer learned that she was a Dismissing Attached adult who felt comfortable with activities, achievements, and plans but not with dependency, closeness and trust. She had to allow herself to experience all these emotions to be empathic to Sacha's feelings, to help him contain his anger, to express his sadness and to help him feel safe in developing closeness to her and the family. Without her changing aspects of her personality Sacha could not have changed his.

Your child can be born with constitutional traits or genetic predispositions but whether the more challenging genes will be activated will also depend on the environment you create. Genes clearly determine whether we will have blue or brown eyes, whether we will be short or tall, whether we will have a cute turned up nose or a large flat nose, how many toes and fingers we will have and many other physical characteristics. These are clearly predetermined by our genetic makeup. Genes may also influence aspects of our personality, but these genes can be modified or not triggered into development because other aspects of our environment are strong influences on genetic development. These can be positive or negative. An infant may be born with an easy-going predisposition but, if this infant experiences trauma early in his or her life from a caregiver, this experience will affect the development of the genetic predisposition. Similarly, an infant may be born dysregulated and tense but, if the caregiver is consistently patient and nurturing, this infant may learn to relax and regulate emotions and behaviour. The influence of the environment on genetics is called epigenetics.

Epigenetics plays its more significant role in early childhood experiences because the brain is rapidly developing and can influence how and whether genes will release their directions for development or will be modified and influenced by the early experiences. The genes we inherit do not have to express themselves or are not set in stone if they are developed. Genes for unhealthy development can be modified by a healthy relationship with caregivers.

How does Adult Attachment play into genetics and epigenetics? Parents with Secure/Autonomous attachments are most likely to provide the safe, nurturing, and predictable environment for infants and to not personalize the normal and more stressful challenges of parenting an infant. An infant may be born genetically predisposed to be more colicky and less able to settle. The infant may cry frequently and for long periods because of this discomfort. This infant will have a greater opportunity to shift this genetic determination with a Securely Attached parent who has the ability to remain calm and patient, consistently soothing her/his infant. This parent will be able to do this because he or she does not personalize the infant's behaviour and does not feel her/his infant is deliberately torturing the parent. This parent will also be able to seek help and support from others when he or she does feel overwhelmed and exhausted.

The parent with a Preoccupied Adult Attachment who is dysregulated, will have a much more challenging time creating the placid environment for the same child. The Preoccupied parent may be caring and nurturing but this is dependent on the parent feeling the infant is responding positively. If the infant cannot be soothed and the Preoccupied parent feels inadequate, this parent will be angry and rejecting of the infant. The Preoccupied parent may turn to others for help, but this would be presented in an angry demanding manner, perhaps alienating the helper. The Preoccupied parent may feel ambivalent about the helper if they are successful in soothing the child, becoming angrier at both the infant and helper. The relationship with the Preoccupied parent will reinforce the genetic markers or expressors for dysregulation in the infant.

The parent with a Dismissing Adult Attachment may be able to provide the regulated and structured environment for their dysregulated infant/child but not the empathic responses and soft nurturing this child would need. If the infant continues to be tense and stressed despite the efforts of the parent, the Dismissing parent may eventually feel inadequate and withdraw from the child. Dismissing parents highly value their competency and ability to perform. When this does not occur despite their best efforts, they may become angry or depressed, rejecting the infant and certainly not being emotionally available. The infant may eventually give up signalling its needs and stop crying but their propensity for stress and anxiety remains imbedded in their personalities.

Parents with an Unresolved Adult Attachment will have the greatest challenge with an infant who is tense, stressed and difficult to soothe. Such children may trigger unresolved feelings in the adult parents caused by their own childhood trauma. An Unresolved parent's response will be unpredictable, perhaps frightening and perhaps dangerous for the infant. This is how trauma is passed on through the generations, although it may not be a genetic trait. A dysregulated infant can be abused by a parent whose own abuse remains unresolved. So, the dysregulated infant becomes a traumatized infant although this aspect of their development was not genetically predisposed. Being traumatized at such a young age, this child will have difficulty reversing its perception of self and others, particularly if the child remains with the traumatized caregiver.

Although this chapter places a great deal of pressure on the parent in the determination of the genetic development of the child, research does indicate that secure parenting is the best determinant of the healthy functioning of a child. Children certainly are born with genetic markers for development, and we do know that certain diseases and mental health issues can be genetically predetermined. If you do have a child born with a genetically based health issue, you should not blame yourself and find all the supports available to assist you in raising a challenged child. The more secure you are in your own attachment, the kinder you will be to yourself, the more likely to feel entitled to support and breaks from parenting and the more likely not to personalize your child's behaviour and challenges.

According to the National Council on The Developing Child:

> *"Scientists have discovered that early experiences can determine how genes are tuned on or off and even whether some are expressed at all. Therefore, the experiences children have early in life—and the environments in which they have them—shape their developing brain architecture and strongly affect whether they grow up to be healthy, productive members of society.*[8]*"*

---

8 National Council on The Developing Child, "Early Experiences can Alter Gene Expression and Affect Long Term Development," Working Paper, May 2010.

The research in the field of genetics and epigenetics is new and continues to develop. However, there is already strong evidence of the importance of the interaction between genes and the environment in the understanding of human development and the development of Attachment.

Chapter 12

CONCLUSION

This book has offered you, as parents, an alternative way of understanding why you parent the way you do, based on the theory of Attachment as it applies to adults. The theory of attachment tells us that children will develop a secure attachment or an insecure attachment based on their experience with their parents/caregivers as infants, children, and adolescents. This means that the best way you, as a parent, can ensure your child feels secure and is successful in relationships and in most areas of their life, is to provide a secure, consistent, and loving environment. Attachment theory also tells us that the parents who can best provide a secure environment have a Secure/autonomous Attachment as an adult.

The research, particularly by Dr. Mary Main, demonstrates that if one knows the attachment of the parent one can predict with a high degree of probability the attachment of the child. This means that if a parent has a secure attachment their child is likely to have a secure attachment. If a parent has an insecure attachment their child is likely to also have a similar insecure attachment. The parent unconsciously passes on their attachment through their interaction with the child from infancy onward.

Research also demonstrates that about 60 percent of adults are securely attached.[9] This means that at least 40 percent of the general adult population are insecurely attached. Since most of these adults will be parents, about 40 percent of parents are insecure and will not be able to offer a secure environment in raising their children. This is a concerning statistic.

These statistics should be an impetus for all parents to learn to become securely attached. Or learn how to parent from a conscious perspective of themselves so they provide the elements of a secure parenting environment for their children.

I am a social worker/therapist. I have been interested in Attachment Theory and been offering therapy based on this for over 30 years. I have worked with adopted and biological children with attachment problems. I have helped parents learn and implement the elements that create a secure family environment. Some parents were successful at this, and others were not. I came to believe that the parents, both adoptive and biological, who could not recreate this secure family environment were parents who had significant attachment issues themselves.

This reality directed my interest in learning more about adult attachment, the categories of adult attachment and how these affected adult relationships and parenting. I wrote a book, called It's Attachment, about understanding oneself from an attachment lens and how to change one's attachment to respond in healthier ways in adult relationships. This book is a follow up but directed to parents. It is important that parents also understand their adult attachment category, how their parenting is affected by this attachment and how to change their parenting, so they respond in healthier ways to their children.

---

9 National Council on The Developing Child, "Early Experiences can Alter Gene Expression and Affect Long Term Development," Working Paper, May 2010.

As a therapist, I developed a model of Attachment Focused Therapy that I teach to other therapists. This model is intended to help clients move from an insecure adult attachment to a Secure/Autonomous one. The therapy is typically long term and can be time-consuming and expensive. I strongly believe in this model and do encourage people to engage in such therapy to repair the effect of their early upbringing and emerge feeling more aware of themselves and more secure. There is no doubt that people who do this therapeutic work will be better parents.

However, I wrote this book for parents who are not able to engage in such therapy or who want to help their children while they work on themselves. This book, like the previous one, offers you guidelines on understanding your adult attachment category. It will help you understand how your adult attachment affects your parenting. Best of all it offers you guidelines on how to change your parenting and respond differently to your children, knowing the challenges to you as an insecurely attached parent.

So, whether you are a parent with one of the insecure adult attachment categories, Preoccupied/Anxious Adult Attachment, Dismissing/Avoidant Adult Attachment, or Unresolved/Disorganized Adult Attachment, you can lessen the detrimental effect your insecure adult attachment will have on your children. You can do this by:

- Owning your type of attachment
- Understanding how it operates in your conscious and unconscious awareness,
- Understanding how it influences your interaction with your children,
- Understanding what aspects of your children will be more challenging to you
- Learning what you need to change to ensure you do not transfer your insecure attachment to your children.

Chapters 5-7 in the book offer examples and practical guidelines and interventions for you to implement, based on your adult attachment category. These interventions will help you to be a more empathic and supportive parent.

Chapter 3 of the book describes how neurological development is influenced by the parent's responses to their children. Infants and children become self-regulated when their parents are empathic to their needs and feelings and offer nurturing and calm responses. Self-regulated children and adults are more successful in all aspects of their lives. Chapter 11 introduces the concept of epigenetics which explains that both genes and environment shape our personalities. This means that parents can influence the genetic potential of their children in positive and negative ways.

Other chapters introduce important parenting concepts such as repairing a rift with your child, after a confrontation or need to implement a consequence. Another chapter will help parents appreciate the need to be attuned to your child and presents ways you can assure your child that you do understand what they are feeling and needing.

Chapter 8 discusses the advantages of being a secure parent in the development of our children.

There is no doubt that secure children have an easier time navigating all the challenges of life. They tend to be happier, have good peer relationships and are successful academically, socially and in their extra-curricular activities. Secure children will develop their own interests and believe in their capacity to succeed to the best of their ability. They will have the capacity to be both independent and dependent, able to turn to their parents and other adults when they need support and guidance. They will grow into secure adults and continue to be successful in both relationships and in their pursuits.

We should all wish this for our children. And you as a parent, whether secure or insecure in your own attachment, can make this happen for your children.

I hope this book has been a helpful guide in your journey to be a parent who offers your children a secure parenting experience.

BIBLIOGRAPHY

Books

Arden, John, *Rewire Your Brain*, (2010) New Jersey, John Wiley and Sons,

Atkinson, Leslie & Zucher, Kenneth J., *Attachment and Psychopathology.* (1997), New York, NY, Guilford Press.

Becker-Weidman, Arthur, *Creating Capacity for Attachment*, 2008, Centre for Family Development, Buffalo, New York.

Bennett, Susanne, Nelson, Judith Kay, *Adult Attachment in Clinical Social Work*, (2011), New York, Springer.

Bowlby, John , *A Secure Base*, (1988), New York, NY: Basic Books.

Brown, Daniel, P. & Elliot, David, *Attachment Disturbances in Adults* (2016) New York, W.W. Norton & Co.

Busch, Karl Heinz, *Treating Attachment Disorders*, (2002), New York, Guilford Press.

Cassidy, J. & Shaver, P.R. (ed.) *Handbook of Attachment*, (1999), New York, Guilford Press.

Cassidy, J. & Shaver, P.R, (ed.) *Handbook of Attachment*, (Third Edition), (2018) New York, Guilford Press.

Clinton, Hilary Rodham, *Living History*, (2003), Simon & Schuster, New York.

Couttender, P.M. & Ainsworth, M, "Child Maltreatment & Attachment Theory," in *Child Maltreatment* (1989), Cicchetti, Dante & Carlson, Vicki, New York, NY, Cambridge University Press.

Cozolino, Louis, *The Neuroscience of Human Relationships* (2006) New York, W.W. Norton & Co.

Daniel, Sarah, *Adult Attachment Patterns in a Treatment Context*, (2015) New York, Routledge.

Doidge, Norman, *The Brain that Changes Itself*, (2007) New York, Penguin Books.

Heller, Diane Poole, Levine, Peter, *The Power of Attachment: How to Create Deep and Lasting Relationships* (2019).

Hesse, Erik, "The Adult Attachment Interview, Historical & Current Perspectives," in Cassidy & Shaver, *Handbook of Attachment* (1999), New York, Guilford Press, p. 395-433.

Hughes, Daniel, *Attachment-focused Parenting*, (2009) New York, W.W. Norton & Co.

Hughes, Daniel, *Attachment Focused Family Therapy*, (2007) New York, W.W. Norton & Co.

Johnson, Susan M., *Attachment Theory in Practice*, (2019) Guilford Press, New York.

Johnson, S. & Whiffen, V., *Attachment Processes in Couple and Family Therapy*, (2006) New York, Guilford Press.

Golding, Kim, *Nurturing Attachments*, (2008) Jessica Kingsley Publishers, London.

Kerns, Kathryn & Richardson, Rhonda, *Attachment in Middle Childhood*, (2005), New York, Guilford Press.

Kussin, Annette, *It's Attachment, A New Way of Understanding Yourself and Your Relationships*, (2020), Guernica Editions (MiroLand), Hamilton, ON.

Land, Mary-Jo, *Caring Together*, a guide for parents, foster parents and adoptive parents of children who are in care, (2019) Speaking Volume Books, Flesherton, ON.

Levine, Amir & Heller Rachel S.F., *Attached* (2011) New York, Penguin Group.

Mandelbaum, Toni, *Attachment and Adult Clinical Practice*, (2021), Routledge, New York.

Maunder Robert & Hunter, Jonathon, *Love, Fear and Health*, (2015) University of Toronto Press, Toronto, Buffalo, London.

Milkulincer, Mario & Shaver, Phillip R, *Attachment in Adulthood*, (2016), New York, Guilford Press.

Muller, Robert, *Trauma and the Avoidant Client*, (2010) New York, W.W. Norton & Co.

Newton, Ruth, *The Attachment Connection*, (2008) New Harbinger Publications, California.

Obegi, Joseph and Berant, Ety, *Attachment Theory and Research in Clinical Work with Adults*, (2009) New York, Guilford Press.

Purvis, Karyn, Cross, David R.& Sunshine, Wendy Lyons, *The Connected Child*, (2007), McGraw-Hill Books, New York.

Sable, Pat, *Attachment and Adult Psychotherapy*, (2000), New Jersey, Jason Aronson Inc.

Saltman, Bethany, *Strange Situation, A Mother's Journey into the Science of Attachment*, (2020) Random House Books, New York.

Siegel, Daniel, *Brainstorm, The Power and Purpose of The Teenage Brain*, (2013) Penguin Random House, New York.

Siegel, Daniel, *Mindsight*, (2010) New York, Bantam Books.

Siegel, Daniel & Hartzell, Mary, *Parenting from the Inside Out*, (2003), New York, Penguin Books.

Siegel, Daniel, *The Mindful Brain* (2007) New York W.W. Norton and Co.

Siegel, Daniel & Bryson, Tina Payne, *The Power of Showing up*, (2020) Ballantyne Books, New York.

Siegel, Daniel, *The Whole-Brain Child*, (2011) New York, Delacorte Press.

Simpson, Jeffery & Rhodes, W. Steven, *Attachment Theory and Close Relationships*, (1998) New York, Guilford Press.

Steele, Howard & Steele, Miriam, *Clinical Applications of the Adult Attachment Interview*, (2008), New York, Guilford Press.

Tatkin, Stan, *Wired for Love*, (2011) Oakland, Cal. New Harbinger Publications Inc.

Wallin, David, *Attachment in Psychotherapy*, (2007) New York, Guilford Press.

Articles

Bakermans-Kranenburg, Marian J. van Ijzendoorn, Marinus H., "Attachment, Parenting and Genetics," in Cassidy, Jude & Shaver, Phillip, *Handbook of Attachment*, 2016, Guilford Press, pp.155-179.

Edelstein, Robin, Alexander, Kristen Weede, Shaver, Phillip, Schaaf, Jeenifer, Quas, Jodi, Lovas, Gretchen & Foodman, Fail, "Adult Attachment Style and parental responsiveness during a stressful event," in *Attachment & Human Development*, Volume 6, Issue 1, March 2004, pg. 21.

Firestone, Lisa, "How Your Attachment Style Impacts Your Relationship," *Psychology Today*, Posted online July 30, 2013.

Grey, Ben, "The Meaning of the Child to the Parent," PH.D Thesis, Dept. of Psychology, University of Roehampton, 2013.

Jacobvitz, Debora & Reisz, Samantha, "Disorganized and Unresolved States in Adulthood," *Current Opinion in Psychology*, 2019, 24:172-176, www//sciencedirect.com.

Holmes, Jeremy, "Disorganized Attachment and Borderline Personality Disorder," in *Attachment and Human Development*, Volume 6, no. 2, June 2004.

Kaitz, Marsha, Bar-Haim, Yair, Lehrer and Ephraim Grossman, "Adult attachment style and interpersonal distance," in *Attachment and Human Development*, Volume 6, No.3, Sept 2004, pp. 285-304.

Koren-Karie & Oppenheim, David (Ed.), "Parental Insightfulness: Its role in fostering children's healthy development," in *Attachment and Human Development*, Vol, 20, No.3, June 2018.

Madigan, Sheri, Bakermans-Kranenburg, Marian J., Van Ijendoorn, Marinus H., Moran, Greg, Pederson, David R., Benoit, Diane, "Unresolved States of mind, anomalous parental behavior and disorganized attachment: a review and meta-analysis of a transmission gap," *Attachment and Human Development*, June 2006, 8(2) pp. 89-111.

Main, M., Kaplan, N., Cassidy, J., 1987, "Security in Infancy, Childhood & Adulthood, A Move to the Level of Representation," in Bretherton & Waters, E. Eds. *Growing Points in /Attachment Theory and*

Research Monogram of Society for Research, Child Development 5.0 (1-2) pp. 66-104.

Mikulincer, Mario & Shaver, Phillip, R., "Adult Attachment and Emotion Regulation," in Cassidy, Jude and Shaver, Phillip, *Handbook of Attachment*, 2016, Guilford Press, pp. 507-533.

National Council on the Developing Child, "Early Experiences Can Alter Gene Expression and Affect in Long Term Development," Working Paper 10, May 2010.

O'Sullivan, Patrick, "Breaking Away: A Harrowing True Story of Resilience, Courage and Triumph," *Canada Press*, Oct. 19, 2013.

Riggs, Shelly, "Childhood Emotional Abuse and Attachment System Across the Life Cycle: What Theory and Research Tell Us," *Journal of Aggression, Maltreatment and Trauma* 19, 5-51, 2010, Taylor and Frances Group.

Saltman, Bethany, "Can Attachment Theory Explain All our Relationships," nymag.com/thecut.

Schore, Judith, & Schore Allan, N., "Modern Attachment Theory: The Central Role of Affect Regulation in Development and Treatment," *Clinical Social Work Journal*, (2008) 36:9-20.

Shapiro, Janet R. & Applegate, Jeffrey, "Cognitive Neuroscience, Neurobiology and Affect Regulation: Implication for Clinical Social Work," *Clinical Social Work Journal*, Vol 18, No 1 Spring, 2000.

Shlafer Rebecca, K. Lee Raby, Jamie M. Lawler, Paloma S. Hesemeyer & Glenn I. Roisman (2014): *Longitudinal associations between adult attachment states of mind and parenting quality, Attachment & Human Development*, DOI: 10.1080/ 14616734.2014.962064.

Sroufe, Alan, "Attachment and Development: A prospective, longitudinal study from birth to adulthood, Attachment and Human Development," December 2005, 7 (4), pp. 349-367.

Sroufe, Alan & Siegel, Daniel, "The Verdict is in: The case for Attachment Theory," drdansiegel.com/uploards/1271.

Zeindler, Christine, "Prenatal Maternal Stress," Douglas Mental Health University Institute, Jan.2013, (online article).

Acknowledgements

I wish to thank all the parents and children I have worked with over the years who inspired me to think about my work with them, both my successes and failures. My wish to have been more helpful with some of these families led me to consider what I might have done differently. This desire led me to think more about adult attachment and it's influence on parenting. I regret not having this awareness many years ago as I believe I would have been more helpful to more of the parents who came to me for help. I am grateful that attachment is now my perspective on understanding the issues that parents struggle with, in their desire to comprehend and help their children.

I also want to thank all the people who read my first book and offered praise and encouragement and some critical appraisal. Their responses encouraged me to write my second book, more aware of grammatical errors.

I want to thank all the researchers and clinicians who provided an abundance of knowledge and experience from which I drew, in the writing of this book. I want to thank Dr. Mary Main and her associates, who inspired me to believe in the theory of adult attachment and incorporate this in my clinical work. I also want to thank Dr. Dan Hughes, who was my first mentor in the practical use of attachment in my work with adopted families. Dr. Hughes and the clinicians in our consultation group were a wonderful source of knowledge and support as we all grabbled with working with adoptive families from an attachment lens.

I want to thank Dr. David Pederson and his team for the training in the Adult Attachment Interview. I continue to value that training and now apply my understanding of adult attachment to parenting dynamics.

In particular, I want to think my husband Uri Igra and my daughter Devra Igra for their unwavering support in the writing of my second book. My husband has tolerated my absences during this writing period with stoicism and understanding. He has validated the importance of this book in his own therapeutic work.

My daughter has been my greatest enthusiast in the writing of my book. She has spent long periods of her time reading and editing the book. We are both delighted that all my efforts in encouraging her to be mindful of grammar during her academic years have paid off. I am the benefit of her talents and now trust her editing abilities as she changed the grammar and content of my book.

My daughter and husband are both accomplished therapists.

I want to thank Guernica Editions and Michael Mirolla for publishing my second book and all the support during the publication process.

About the Author

Annette Kussin is a social worker/psychotherapist who has a private practice in Toronto, Ontario, Canada. She has worked much of her career in Children's Mental Health as a front-line worker, supervisor, director of a family therapy program and a clinical director of a number of mental health agencies, which offered services to young children and adolescents. She offered new clinical directions to the agencies and supervised many front-line staff and managers.

Annette eventually left the public sector and started a full time private practice in 1998 in partnership with 2 other therapists. She focused her work on the understanding and treatment of trauma, attachment, and brain development, offering therapy and developing workshops for other professionals. After leaving the partnership Annette and her husband bought and managed a private therapy centre, called The Leaside Therapy Centre. The Centre offered multi-discipline services and provided a community of therapists to both the public and professionals. Annette had an active private practice at the Centre, providing therapy, consultation, and training. After almost a decade Annette and her husband sold the Centre. Annette has continued her private practice, specializing in attachment focused therapy. She now offers many workshops in this area and provides supervision and consultation to other professionals and agencies.

Annette's interest in child and adult attachment grew out of her work with adopted children and their parents. Annette worked with adopted families, using a model of attachment focused therapy, for many years. Annette came to believe that it was the attachment of the parents that influenced the parenting of their adopted children. Parents with insecure attachment had more challenges accepting and not personalizing the behaviour and responses of their children.

Annette felt the need to understand in more depth adult attachment and the different categories of adult attachment. She studied the work of Dr. Mary Main and eventually took a course on scoring the Adult Attachment Interview, a research protocol developed by Dr. Main. She was most interested in applying the categories of adult attachment to clinical work. She began to do this in her clinical work and eventually developed workshops to encourage other professionals to incorporate an understanding of adult attachment in their clinical work. She has offered workshops for many years to many organizations and universities throughout Ontario. She developed an advanced course in adult attachment and offers consultation and supervision to individuals, therapists, and organizations.

In 2020, Annette published her book *Adult Attachment, a New Way of Understanding Yourself and Your Relationships*. Annette's book launch was cancelled due to covid and she has been limited in promoting and selling her book. Despite this, the book has done well and was one of the best sellers at a popular mental health bookstore.

Annette's understanding of adult attachment has confirmed her clinical and personal experience that a parent's adult attachment greatly influences their parenting. Research has long provided evidence of this. In her clinical work Annette attempts to understand the adult attachment category of the parent and help the parents understand how their insecure adult attachment limits their parenting. She offers parents both interventions to help them provide more security for their children and therapy to help them resolve their problematic childhood experiences. Annette's successes in her clinical work steered her to develop workshops on adult attachment and parenting to other professionals. She has been providing these for many years.

Annette has written this book on adult attachment and parenting, called *Secure Parent, Secure Child*, because of her belief that parents also need to have this perspective on themselves and their parenting struggles. There are many books on parenting but this one is unique in its focus on how a parent's adult attachment influences their parenting, whether they are secure or insecure in their adult attachment. The book offers interventions for parents and the hopeful understanding that even insecure parents can produce securely attached children. With an awareness of their adult attachment and changing the unhealthy parenting practices that attachment insecurities bring, all parents can provide the elements of a secure safe environment.

Perhaps the title of this book should be *Insecure Parents, Secure Children.*

Printed in January 2023
by Gauvin Press,
Gatineau, Québec